Antonin Artaud : WORKS ON PAPER

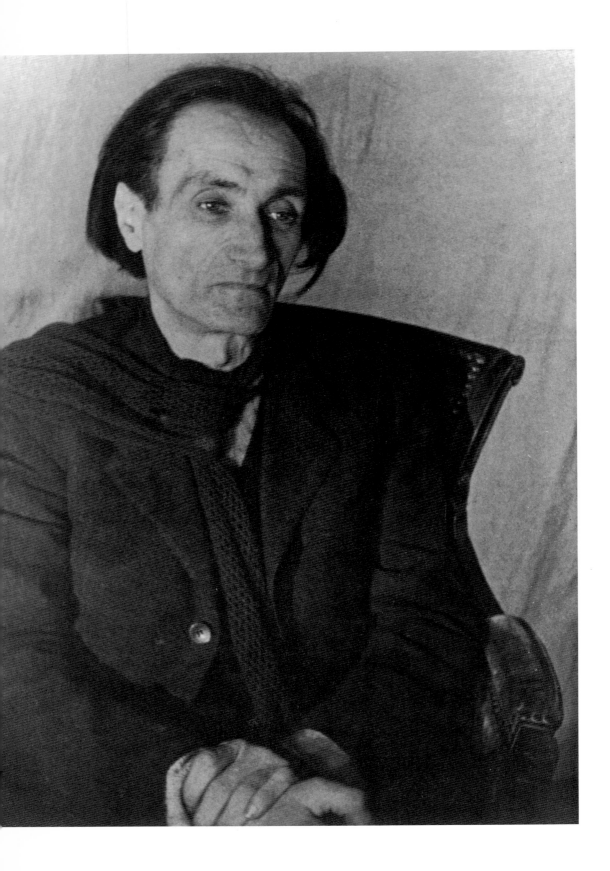

Antonin Artaud

WORKS ON PAPER

EDITED BY

MARGIT ROWELL

THE MUSEUM OF MODERN ART, NEW YORK

DISTRIBUTED BY HARRY N. ABRAMS, INC., NEW YORK

Published in conjunction
with the exhibition
*Antonin Artaud:
Works on Paper* at
The Museum of Modern Art,
New York, October 3, 1996,
to January 7, 1997.
The exhibition was organized
by Margit Rowell,
Chief Curator,
Department of Drawings,
The Museum of Modern Art,
New York.

Produced by the
Department of Publications
The Museum of Modern Art,
New York
Osa Brown,
Director of Publications
Edited by Christopher Lyon
Designed by J. Abbott Miller,
Paul Carlos—Design/
Writing/Research
Production by Marc Sapir
Printed by Stamperia
Valdonega, Verona, Italy
Bound by Legatoria Torriani
Milan, Italy

Library of Congress
Catalogue Card Number
96-75940

ISBN 0-87070-118-5
(MoMA)

ISBN 0-8109-6168-7
(Abrams)

Distributed in the
United States and Canada by
Harry N. Abrams, Inc.,
New York
A Times Mirror Company

Printed in the United States
of America

Cover: Antonin Artaud,
passport photograph, 1944.

Frontispiece: Antonin
Artaud, 1946. Photographed
by Denise Colomb.

CONTENTS

Foreword

Antonin Artaud, who died almost fifty years ago, remains one of this century's more compelling— and complicated—literary figures, a man of enormous talent and insight whose disturbed and often difficult life inflected almost every aspect of his work. Troubled by mental illness and addicted to drugs, he explored his inner world through poetry and prose, creating a body of material whose haunting depictions of alienation, trauma, and pain have few parallels. Best known for his "Theater of Cruelty," a project based on his vision of cruelty as truth and as a transforming experience, Artaud was also an accomplished artist whose drawings record the harrowing images that populated his mind.

Comprising approximately seventy works on paper, this exhibition provides the first opportunity in this country to examine the full extent of Artaud's graphic work. Highly charged and expressive, as intense as they are personal, these strange incantations and spells, fragmented images, and penetrating portraits offer a glimpse of Artaud's world, particularly his obsessions with death, sexuality, and identity. The sheer visual force of these drawings, with their rubbed surfaces, burn marks, smears, and staccato bursts of line and color, distinguishes them from the work of other artists and reveals his unique voice.

Artaud's suffering and anguish remind us of Vincent van Gogh, with whom Artaud identified closely. He, too, underwent extensive treatment for his illness, suffered long confinement, but never knew the comfort of a cure. He shared van Gogh's sense of existing outside the normal boundaries or constraints of society, resulting in profound alienation and isolation from the world. Like van Gogh, he experienced fits of erratic behavior that gave way to periods in which he was able to create images of transcendent power from the depths of his experiences, and, as with van Gogh, these bursts of creativity were, paradoxically, often accompanied by moments of terrifying torment, self-loathing, and anguish. In their alienation and suffering, both men have become emblematic of the modern artist at odds with the world.

Although these drawings ultimately must be seen in the broad context of Artaud's complicated and disturbed life, and in relation to his extraordinary literary output, they also can be appreciated for what they are: discrete works of art, often of great power and beauty. And while Artaud's literary genius was recognized—if not fully appreciated—during his lifetime, it is only recently that his legacy as a visual artist has become clear. Margit Rowell, Chief Curator, Department of Drawings, has worked tirelessly on this exhibition, and her insightful essay on Artaud in this publication, combined with her selection of drawings to be shown, reflect her commitment to the artist. Finally, I wish to thank Germain Viatte, Director, Musée National d'Art Moderne, Centre Georges Pompidou, Paris, and Bernard Blistène, former Director of the Musées de Marseille, without whose generous cooperation this project would not have been possible.

Glenn D. Lowry
Director, The Museum of Modern Art

Preface

Few graphic expressions in the twentieth century show the power and authentic inner necessity seen in the drawings of Antonin Artaud. Executed between 1937 and early 1948, years when Artaud was mostly confined in various psychiatric institutions in France or under medical supervision, these drawings are no more the creation of an alienated personality than is the prolific outpouring of written expression that he produced simultaneously and for which he is internationally celebrated. Instead they show the heightened sensibility and critical lucidity of a mind at odds with society and unable to compromise with its conventions. These works have come to public attention in France only within the last decade and have not been seen in the United States. As they are a distinctive phenomenon of our time, it appeared urgent to show them to an American audience before this century comes to a close.

Despite its modest scale, this exhibition of Artaud's drawings demanded the energy and commitment of many people to whom I wish to extend my thanks. First, I join Glenn Lowry in thanking Germain Viatte, without whose enthusiastic support and facilitation of the loan of a large group of works, the exhibition could not have taken place. Also at the Musée National d'Art Moderne, I am grateful to Marie-Laure Bernadac, Chief Curator of the Department of Drawings, for generously agreeing to these loans, and to Jean-Paul Oddos, Head of the Service de Documentation, for his contribution of documentary material. My thanks go as well to Bernard Blistène for agreeing to lend works from the Musée Cantini, Marseille. Nicolas Cendo, Curator at the Musée Cantini, was helpful in securing these and several other loans. But my deepest gratitude goes to Agnès de la Beaumelle, Curator at the Musée National d'Art Moderne, for her commitment to this project, her knowledge and guidance, and her negotiation of several delicate loans. Her introductions to the three periods of Artaud's drawing activity represented in the plate section of this publication are a valuable contribution to our understanding of the drawings' complexity.

Although most of the lenders have preferred to remain anonymous, we hope that they will hereby accept our sincerest gratitude for their participation in this project. We also wish to thank Mme. Florence Loeb, for her generous contributions to the success of our endeavor, as well as Jean Favier, President, and Florence de Lussy, Chief Curator of Manuscripts, Bibliothèque Nationale de France, Paris; Michèle Gendreau-Massaloux, Rector of the Université de Paris Sorbonne; and Yves Peyré, Director of the Bibliothèque Littéraire Jacques Doucet, Paris, without whose assistance in many areas we could not have hoped for the richness of documentation and representation present in the exhibition and this volume.

The book is dedicated to Marthe Robert. More than any other contributor to this endeavor, she represented a living link between myself and Antonin Artaud, the man and his work. Unfortunately, she did not live to see the project's completion, but the simplicity and generosity with which she evoked him, in her conversation and her writings, made the myth come alive for those who were not privileged to know him. The concept of the book was partly inspired by Sylvère Lotringer, Professor of French Literature at Columbia University, whose total commitment to this project as an advisor, colleague, and friend was indispensable to the Museum's curatorial staff; to him we extend our sincerest gratitude. Serge Malaussèna, Artaud's nephew, who was generous with time and information, allowed us to publish here for the first time a largely unknown text. We are grateful for his support of this project. Furthermore, we thank Ronald Hayman, Kiki Smith, Patti Smith, and Nancy Spero for their contributions, and Jeanine Herman, Roger McKeon, and Richard Sieburth for their translations from the French. Other sources of aid and assistance include Erick Bergquist, Victor Bouillon, Jacques Faujour, Véronique Legrand, and Christiane Rojouan. Finally we would like to express our enthusiasm to J. Abbott Miller of Design/Writing/Research for his imaginative book design.

It goes without saying that many members of The Museum of Modern Art's staff contributed to the realization of this project with unstinting collegiality and efficiency: we thank Peter Galassi, Chief Curator, Department of Photography, and Janis Ekdahl, Acting Director, Library, for loans from their respective departments; in the Department of Publications we thank Osa Brown, Director, Harriet Schoenholz Bee, Managing Editor, and Marc Sapir, Assistant Production Manager, for moral and technical support in the book's production, and Christopher Lyon, Editor, whose sensitive, intelligent, and meticulous attention to the publication's content went far beyond a purely editorial task.

Richard L. Palmer, Coordinator of Exhibitions, Jerome Neuner, Director of Exhibition Design and Production, Beverly M. Wolff, Secretary and General Counsel, Stephen W. Clark, Assistant General Counsel, Eumie Imm Stroukoff, Associate Librarian, Lucille Stiger, Assistant Registrar, Michael Margitich, Deputy Director for Development, Brett Cobb, Director of Development and Membership, Jody Hanson, Director, Department of Graphics, and Holly Goetz, Coordinator/Assistant to the Chief Curator, Department of Drawings, all helped us to see this project through. Christina Houstian, Curatorial Assistant, Department of Drawings, deserves particular thanks and recognition for her contributions to the publication's documentary matter and for overseeing many tasks pertaining to the exhibition and book, all carried out with supreme intelligence and unruffled good humor.

Finally, I would like to express my gratitude to Glenn Lowry, Director of the Museum, for his unfailing belief in the significance of this project and his enthusiastic commitment and support.

Margit Rowell
Chief Curator, Department of Drawings

To Marthe Robert
(1914–1996)

Antonin Artaud, 1947.
Photographed by Georges Pastier.

Images of Cruelty: The Drawings of Antonin Artaud

Margit Rowell

In 1932 Antonin Artaud published the first of two theoretical writings that would make him famous, the texts cited before all others, his "Theater of Cruelty" manifestos. Therein he proclaimed that the theater must provide "the spectator with the truthful precipitates of dreams, in which his taste for crime, his erotic obsessions, his savagery, his fantasies, his utopian sense of life and of things, even his cannibalism, pour out on a level that is not counterfeit and illusory but internal. . . . the theater, like dreams, is bloody and inhuman."[1]

In 1945 Artaud embarked on a series of drawings in which it would seem that these criteria were his guiding principles. The fractured and disjunctive images are indeed nightmarish and obsessional, and bespeak the denial of a culture of reason, which underlies all Artaud's pronouncements. The first group of drawings would be followed by a sequence of portraits, begun upon his transfer to Ivry in 1946, in which, despite the more conventional artistic genre, an analogous "cruelty" is manifest. These two series represent the prime constituents of Artaud's graphic production.

This graphic activity was not unprecedented in Artaud's history. He had painted and drawn as a child and as a young man, and even had shown a respectable amount of talent. Though his youthful paintings and sketches can hardly be seen to relate to the physical and emotional violence of the later works, there was a period and a production that signaled what was to come: the signs are evident in the spells (*sorts*), triggered by his ill-fated trip to Ireland, which Artaud elaborated and sent to friends and imagined acquaintances in 1937 to 1939. This trip marked a turning point in Artaud's mental health and his destiny. High-strung since early youth and beset with nervous disorders, he

1
Selected Writings, 244–45. The principal sources of texts by Artaud are abbreviated in the notes. See Select Bibliography, p. 164, for full citations of principal sources.

developed, at the age of forty-one, a form of paraphrenia or schizophrenia, and from that time forward, his creative output was of a different character and content. It is important to note that Artaud's illness has never been definitively diagnosed. Although some of his doctors declared him schizophrenic—the term which appears in most of the literature—it is more probable that he, like Gérard de Nerval, suffered from confabulatory paraphrenia, a delusional psychosis which is not accompanied by intellectual deterioration and in which some symptoms—hallucinations and confabulations—are close to those of schizophrenia.

The spells are not drawings in the accepted sense. Handwritten letters to friends or imaginary acquaintances, they were intended to curse, warn, or protect their recipients. However they do exhibit highly eccentric graphic incident: the writing is sometimes punctuated with cabalistic signs; and, as though accidentally but clearly with intention, the pages are torn and punctured, burned, smeared, and splotched with ink and gouache. Here Artaud's contention that words were not adequate to project his incantatory message is made vividly clear. As we recall, verbal language for Artaud corresponded to a fabric of conventions; it was always someone else's language, not one's own voice. Indeed, Artaud's vehemence is transmitted by the spells as much through their visual impact as in the messages of their texts.

During the initial years of Artaud's internment at Rodez, he wrote very little, with the exception of letters to his family, his friends, and his doctors, and he did not draw. Although he had written and published extensively throughout the 1920s and 1930s, on his arrival at Rodez, he was psychologically blocked. The electroshock treatment, decried by many of his exegetes (and by Artaud himself), seems to have unlocked if not fostered a new creativity: one cannot fail to be impressed by the extraordinary perceptions and erudition apparent in the torrential flow of texts and letters which he began to produce. From 1945 until his death in early 1948, his output was prodigious: his writings, often punctuated or interrupted by sketches of varying degrees of legibility, fill the pages of 406 notebooks. But for Artaud, none of this writing was *literature*, which to his eyes connoted an artificial or "counterfeit" idiom or convention: expression mediated by style. On the contrary, although he did not call it such, his writings are a kind of extended journal or diary, the expression of his true being—not art, just being.

At Rodez, Dr. Gaston Ferdière encouraged him to draw again. By this time, the diagnosis of schizophrenia had been made, and it is tempting to interpret the drawings done at Rodez, with their hallucinatory images, disconnected phrases, words, or truncated syllables, totally dissociated spaces and motifs, explicitly sexual and scato-logical content, and dense crowding or *horror vacui*, according to clinically defined criteria. But the drawings instead must be seen as Artaud's attempt (as he would later say of van Gogh) to lay "bare the body of man, beyond the subter-fuges of the mind."[2] More specifically, for those familiar with Artaud's personal obsessions, it is clear that he was exorcizing his personal demons and nightmares concerning religion, sexuality, birth and death, torture, war, electroshock therapy, and so on. The form of his expression, dictated by his desire to project the unadulterated emotions of the spiritual-organic, now dissociated, self, was a hieroglyphic (a term Artaud favored for its nonverbal, symbolic connotations) sign language.

As for the handwritten notations, they are relatively, although not totally, obscure as to their content and function. While Artaud's illness may not have been clinical schizophrenia, Gilles Deleuze's analysis of schizophrenic language in relation to Artaud provides useful insights for understanding the presence and formulation of the notations: "The duality of schizophrenic words . . . consists of *passion-words which explode*

3
Gilles Deleuze, "The Schizophrenic and Language: Surface and Depth in Lewis Carroll and Antonin Artaud," in Josue Harari, ed., *Textual Strategies: Perspectives in Post-Structuralist Criticism* (Ithaca: Cornell, 1979), 291.

2
Selected Writings, 509.

4
Jacques Prevel, *En compagnie d'Antonin Artaud* (Paris: Flammarion, 1974), 48.

in wounding phonetic values, and *action-words which weld together inarticulated tonic values.* These two types of words develop in relation to the state of the body, which is either fragmented or organless. They also refer to two types of theater—the theater of terror and passion, and the theater of cruelty, which [are] essentially active—as well as to two types of non-sense, passive and active: the non-sense of words emptied of meaning, which decompose into phonetic elements, and the non-sense of tonic elements, which form indecomposable words that are no less empty. In both these cases everything happens below meaning, far from the surface."[3] Thus the drawings' dissociated images and detached linguistic units derive from the same psychological framework, from the depths of the disintegrated self.

While sketchy portraits and self-portraits are sometimes found in the notebooks and in the Rodez drawings, Artaud's first attempts to con-ceive a portrait as such seem to date from May 1946, shortly before his release from Rodez and his transfer to Ivry. The first two examples appear transitional: *The Blue Head* (undated) and a self-portrait, dated 11 May 1946. In contrast to many of the earlier works on paper, relatively loosely organized and drawn, as though the hand were guided in a state of trance, these images are heavily worked and reworked. The smudged shading, incisive lines, and modelling and punc-turing of the facial skin add a strongly physical dimension to the metaphysical torments that inform them.

In *The Blue Head* (cat. no. 33), the horror transmitted by the rolled-back eyes, flared nos-trils, and exaggerated opening of the mouth set in an elongated oval face is further accentuated by the pockmarks, sores, and bruises of the muti-lated skin, and the tremulous vibrations of the head, recoiling in helpless terror. The poet Jacques Prevel, upon discovering this portrait, would write in his diary: "I was also struck by a large head, with the eyes rolled back, an atro-ciously deformed face, and the hair like a shower of blood."[4]

The Blue Head appears as the symbolic portrait of an inarticulate shriek or cry, originating in a mass of flesh. Once again, Deleuze's penetrating analysis of Artaud in relation to schizophrenia is illuminating: "the first evidence of schizophrenia is that the surface is punctured. Bodies no longer have a surface. The schizophrenic body appears as a kind of body-sieve. Freud emphasized this schizophrenic aptitude for perceiving the surface and the skin as if each were pierced with an infinite number of little holes. As a result, the entire body is nothing but depth; . . . As there is no surface, interior and exterior, container and content no longer have precise limits. . . . Body-sieve, fragmented body, and dissociated body form the first three dimensions of the schizophrenic body—they give evidence of the general breakdown of surfaces."5

Deleuze continues, still in relation to Artaud, saying that in "this breakdown of surface," words, which are surface formulations or conventions, lose part of their power to designate, express, or signify. And it follows that the only valid language is an inarticulate, physical language, where words are decomposed into syllables and sounds, and expelled by the body in a "vocal outburst," a shriek or cry.6

The second symbolic portrait (cat. no. 32) is his first known self-portrait from this period. Dr. Jean Dequeker, an intern at Rodez, recalled in 1959: "During a period of several days, I witnessed the grinding out of this image, the savage hammering out of a form which was not his own. On a large sheet of white paper, he had drawn the abstract contours of a face and in that barely sketched-out mass where he had placed the blackened areas of future interventions, without a mirror, I saw him create his double, distilled as from a crucible, at the price of a torment and a cruelty beyond expression. He worked in a rage, breaking one crayon after another, suffering the internal tortures of his own exorcism. All the while shrieking and reciting feverish poems which arose from the depths of his martyr's soul, he struck and chanted to a population of rebel larvae when suddenly reality appeared to him, in the form of his own face.

"This was the horrible lucidity of Artaud creating himself. . . . And when this face had become the symbolic identity of his own face,

when its black mass was spread out before him like an object of fascination, . . . with the creative rage with which he had blasted open the bolts of reality, as well as those of the surreal, I saw him blindly gouge the eyes of his own image.

"For this, to him, was to be a visionary: by passing through the depth of his own eyes, to perceive the reality on the other side."7

Although this is one of the few extensive eyewitness accounts of Artaud in the act of making a portrait, other testimonies concur that he often (if not always) worked in a state of extreme excitement, pounding the paper, breaking his pencils, tearing the sheet with his rabid gestures. This self-portrait is somewhat unique in relation to his other self-portraits, both in the physically mutilated and spiritually stigmatized vision coerced from inchoate matter, and the incantatory nature of its genesis. In a sense one might say that in these two early portraits, with no models to guide him, Artaud was attempting to plumb the abyss of his own self so completely as to obtain that which is beyond representation, "the reality on the other side."

The subsequent portraits, starting around August 1946 and extending to December 1947, are less aggressively cruel in their portrayals and execution, less fraught with internal violence and pain. It should be remembered that Artaud was no longer institutionalized, and thus isolated, as he had been at Rodez, and was free to come and go at Ivry, so that this period marks his return to a social milieu. Presumably, he began to show interest in doing portraits of friends. Nonetheless, truth, as he put it, the authentic self of the sitter, not surface beauty, was his objective. These portraits manifest quite clearly the extreme subjectivity and the ironic objectivity which characterize certain states of madness as well as dreams.8 In their incisive exploration of the other, they show a subtle sliding from surface into depth, from the container to the contained.

The scattered phrases or shattered "glossolalia," integral to many of the Rodez drawings, are absent from most of the portraits. Although many of the the written texts here are again unintelligible, others manifest an explicit preoccupation in regard to the model.

5 Deleuze, 286–87.

6 Ibid., 287.

7 *Antonin Artaud: Oeuvres sur papier* (Marseille: Musée Cantini, 1995), 158.

8 See Michel Foucault, *Histoire de la folie* (Paris: Gallimard, 1972), 536.

For example, the message inscribed on the portrait of Jacques Prevel (cat no. 44) is a clear admonition from Artaud to Prevel, concerning his "Sin," or sexual activity, with Jany de Ruy—sexuality, as opposed to purity, being one of Artaud's constant obsessions.

These portraits, started in front of the model and usually finished from memory, are in one sense more academic than the previous series of drawings. They show technical skill and an ability to capture and interpret physical resemblance and psychology. Some are torturously reworked: the contours are obsessively repeated, the details erased and redrawn, the soft pencil gouging the surface. Others convey an aloofness, suggesting a subjective or emotional distance from the sitter at that particular moment.

Certain automatisms, repetitions, and a consistent awkwardness suggest a ritual activity as opposed to an artistic intent: the relation of image to sheet (often uncentered, high, isolated), the repeated convention for the neck as a truncated stub, the scrubby treatment of the hair. From portrait to portrait, Artaud does not attempt to improve his technique, to progress, or to perfect his drawing style. On the contrary, his objective was to burrow ever deeper under the skin, behind the facade, and to reveal psychological or mystical truths which were only his to see. As he said, "My drawings are not drawings but documents."[9] Instead of drawings, then, these must be seen as effigies in which the articulations between concealment and disclosure, the flesh and the spirit, inner suffering and the outer shell, are invisible, fused in a seamless and charged presence.

Although most of Artaud's writings are now available to the French-reading public in the twenty-eight volumes published by Gallimard, and selections have been available in English, Artaud's drawings have only occasionally been seen as a body and have been relatively little studied.[10] It must be said that the context within which they might be examined is problematic. Whereas it is clear that they cannot be totally dissociated from his biography or from his written oeuvre, their extraordinary expressive impact forces us to acknowledge them on their

own terms. This being said, it is difficult to compare them to the work of other artists of any given period, including Artaud's own.

Briefly, from 1924 to 1926, Artaud participated in the Surrealist movement, but his radical independence and his uncontrollable personality, perpetually in revolt, brought about his excommunication by André Breton. Moreover, during the 1920s, although Artaud was intensely involved with theater, film, and poetry, he made few drawings. And although he was present at séances of automatic writing, it is doubtful that his writings or later drawings were affected by the experience.

By the late 1930s he was dependent on drugs to relieve his constant pain, and beset by paraphrenia. His writings betray a visionary depth and a poetic clarity which at one time would have been difficult to correlate with madness, yet which the twentieth century has come to recognize as symptomatic of an extreme pathological state. Other writers, thinkers, and artists of renown who also have been subject to depression, hallucinations, and differing degrees of psychosis include Hölderlin, Nietzsche, Nerval, and van Gogh, with all of whom Artaud identified at some point in his writings. Yet their claim to genius has not been tarnished by knowledge of their illnesses. Quite the contrary, it is by now commonly accepted that such forms of illness reorganized as they disorganized these thinkers' vision and its expression. It is furthermore significant that Jean Dubuffet, who was constituting his collection of *art brut* at the very time he met Artaud in 1945, was careful to distinguish between Artaud's drawings and those of the clinically insane. And in fact, between Dubuffet's collection and Artaud's drawings, no comparisons may be made.

Artaud's most literal identification was with van Gogh, based on the conviction that a unique visionary such as he, a man of such purity and innocence, and besieged, like himself, with chronic physical and mental pain, could only be misunderstood, and unjustly sacrificed or "suicided" by society.[11] Artaud identified with van Gogh's sensitivity and extreme clairvoyance, situating them at the borderline between

9 See "Mes dessins ne sont pas des dessins . . . ," pp. 61–62.

10 See Exhibition History and Select Bibliography, pp. 163–64.

11 See *Van Gogh, the Man Suicided by Society* in *Selected Writings*, 483–512.

unreason and reason, dementia and health, chaos and order, innocence and purity as opposed to social convention, nakedness as opposed to inhibition, life as opposed to anesthesia or the living death imposed by false ideas of culture. Like van Gogh, Artaud's destiny was to walk on the edge, the edge of the abyss. This was his understanding of the vocation of the artist, "to see farther, infinitely and dangerously farther, than the immediate and apparent reality of facts . . . farther in his consciousness than consciousness usually contains."[12]

Artaud, too, was a victim of his destiny, by which his extraordinary gifts became a curse and transformed his very existence into a calvary. Yet like van Gogh, even more than van Gogh, his singular itinerary produced an oeuvre of profound significance and infinite resonance for future generations of writers, performers, and artists throughout the world. His descent into hell was in fact a flight from the living hell of his day-by-day existence, engendered by the narrow strictures of a bourgeois, rational world.

Artaud's universal appeal derives not only from what he had to say but from whence it came; his was a voice from the other side. His illness, although it helps to explain his exacerbated sensitivity, his visionary insights, the patterns and functions of his expression, and the prodigious abundance of his oeuvre, is not the key to his genius. Despite the state of inviolate innocence which is commonly attributed to both genius and madness, and which was the ultimate goal of Artaud's perpetual revolt, the workings of pathology and genius are not exactly synonymous. And yet it might be said that for players from both arenas, the tortuous game of creativity is played according to the same rules and the cards are the same. However, in madness, the cards (of the composite organic-spiritual body) are reshuffled, redealt, and the stakes are as

[12] *Selected Writings*, 494.

[13] Michel Foucault, *Madness and Civilization* (New York: Vintage Books, 1973), 288–89.

high as life itself. This is the only difference, but it is fundamental to the substantive nature of the exercise, if not to its outcome. For the outcome, in both cases, is totally unpredictable. And often, but this is of little consolation to the player, it is he who loses who may emerge victorious in the long run, opening up the game by irreversibly reordering its rules.

As Michel Foucault has expressed it, "by the madness which interrupts it, a work of art opens a void, a moment of silence, a question without answer, provokes a breach without reconciliation where the world is forced to question itself. . . . Henceforth, and through the mediation of madness, it is the world that becomes culpable . . . in relation to the work of art; it is now . . . obliged to order itself by its language, compelled by it to a task of recognition, of reparation, to the task of restoring reason *from* that unreason and *to* that unreason. . . . The moment when, together, the work of art and madness are born and fulfilled is the beginning of the time when the world finds itself arraigned by that work of art and responsible before it for what it is."[13]

Artaud, in his desperate attempt to reclaim a natural voice, natural truths, found a refuge from his intenable present in a mythical past. More specifically, by the notion of aggressive cruelty which inspired and informed his life, his writings, and these drawings, he transgressed the established conventions of society, transformed the traditional language of creative expression, and sought to redefine all cultural experience and its place in the world. His profound influence on contemporary culture is sufficient to recognize that from the game he lost in his tragic existence, his voice emerged victorious. And this is ample justification for honoring and exhibiting these drawings, these images of cruelty, the graphic representation or double of his arraignment of the world.

1
Self-Portrait
c. 1915
Charcoal
5⅞ x 4" (15 x 10 cm)
Private collection

Antonin Artaud

Ronald Hayman

The best writers, according to Nietzsche, are men whose "thinking constitutes the involuntary biography of a soul." No one has pointed more insistently than he did to the interdependence of mood and insight, neurosis and statement, sickness and vision. He was a lifelong sufferer from headaches, dyspepsia, nausea, insomnia, and pains in the throat, but he believed that only sick men are in a position to write about health. Most of us take physical well-being for granted except when we're deprived of it. To understand what it felt like to be Friedrich Nietzsche—or Antonin Artaud—we must remember that for them malaise was the norm.

Malaise is conducive to self-examination, and, like Nietzsche, Artaud not only read his own sick body as if it were a map of the universe but saw himself as capable of biting into the tumor that was devouring him and using the poison therapeutically on a cancerous culture. In 1923, at the age of twenty-seven, he told his psychiatrist Dr. Édouard Toulouse: "What you take to be my works are now, as in the past, nothing except waste matter from myself, scrapings off the soul, which the normal man doesn't collect."[1]

When some of his verse was rejected by Jacques Rivière, editor of *La Nouvelle Revue Française*, he began to write prose poems that continued the self-analysis he'd begun in letters to doctors and resumed in letters to Rivière. His art had become secondary to his life, which became more like a work of art or a myth. He'd have done anything to escape the pain and discomfort that dogged him, but unable to shake them off, he cultivated his reactions. Abandoning poems without being able to mold them into a form he found satisfying, he diagnosed in a 1924 letter to Rivière "a central collapse of the soul . . . a kind of erosion, both essential and fleeting, of the thought . . . a temporary non-possession of

NOTE: *Citations in this essay of Artaud's* Oeuvres complètes *refer to the first edition (Paris: Editions Gallimard, 1956–76), except references to vol. 1, where the first revised edition was used. Texts are by Artaud unless otherwise noted.*

2
Selected Writings, 34–35.

1
O.C. 1, bk. 2, 103–4. See Select Bibliography, p. 164, for full citations of principal sources.

3
"Je n'ai jamais rien étudié" (1945), *84,* no. 16.

the material benefits of my development . . . There is something which destroys my thought . . . which robs me of the words *that I have found,* which reduces my mental tension, which is gradually destroying in its substance the body of my thought."[2]

Even as a child he had difficulties in expressing himself. His stammering may have originated in his troubled relationship with his mother. A Levantine Greek married to her cousin, a shipping agent, Euphrasie Artaud bore nine children, but only three survived infancy, and at four Antonin was ill with what may have been meningitis. At the family home in Marseille, his father was seldom present, and he was mostly surrounded by females, including his surviving grandmother, sister of the one who had died. Like his mother, they oscillated between tenderness and strictness. He was fed with Greek pastries and dosed with unpalatable medicines. His powders were sometimes mixed with jam, and he couldn't always distinguish between pain inflicted to punish him and pain caused by sickness. Nor could he always tell whether the source was internal or external. "What is this self," he wrote later, "that experiences what's called being—being a being because I have a body? Mr. Habits, Mr. Nausea, Mr. Revulsion, Mr. Cramps, Mr. Dizziness, Mr. Spanking, and Mr. Slaps keep pace with Mr. Disobedient, Mr. Reaction, Mr. Tears, Mr. Choked in a scandalized soul to make up the self of a child."[3]

Nothing in his childhood was stable; reassurance was tentative and temporary. Stammering and terrifying contractions in the facial nerves and tongue alternated with periods of tranquility. But as an adult he couldn't remember loving his father, and it was only when the old man died that Antonin could forgive him for "this inhuman harshness he trod me down with . . . And I, who am embarrassed at my body, understood that throughout his life he'd been embarrassed with his body, and that there's a lie in existence which we're born to resist."[4]

His mother seemed to be providing his identity, just as she'd provided his nickname, Nanaqui. In adult relationships he clung to it, often signing letters with it. But for the verse he published in a school magazine he adopted the romantic pseudonym Louis des Attides. Reading and writing began to offer an alternative space he could inhabit, but it was precarious. At about eighteen he tried to destroy everything he'd written and to get rid of all his books. When the crisis was over, he was sent to a sanatorium near Marseille. In 1916 he was healthy enough to pass an army physical, but after nine months of military service he was released, and for years he was shunted from one clinic to another: to Saint-Dizier, near Lyons, to Lafoux-les-Bains, to Divonne-les-Bains, and to Bagnères-de-Bigorre before he spent two years at a Swiss clinic near Neuchâtel. There, the medical director, Dr. Dardel, recommended Dr. Toulouse, a progressive psychiatrist who believed in the therapeutic value of literature. He quickly spotted the talent of his new patient, who contributed poems, articles, and reviews of plays and art exhibitions to the review *Demain*, which the doctor edited.

It was thanks to Dr. Toulouse that Artaud got his first job in the theater. Introduced in 1920 to Aurélien-Marie Lugné-Poë, director of the Théâtre de l'Oeuvre, he was offered a small part in Henri de Régnier's play *Les Scrupules de Sganarelle*. Though vain about his good looks and excited about appearing on stage, he soon adopted a quasi-religious attitude to theater. He wanted to make statements about the inner life, statements depending less on words than on atmosphere, gesture, décor, costume, pageantry, music. Becoming a congregation, the audience should react in a way that was partly unconscious, partly physical, perhaps partly spiritual. Two years earlier, at the age of twenty-two, he'd conceived a project for "spontaneous theater," created by a roving troupe of actors performing in factories.

By then he was dependent on drugs, including opiates, for the relief of pain, and he couldn't

tell whether they were robbing him of the words he'd found, slackening his mental tension, and unraveling his thought processes—the complaints he diagnosed in the 1924 letter to Rivière. At the end of 1925 he wanted "to be caught up in the works of a new, an absolute force of gravity. For me it's like an overwhelming reorganization determined only by the laws of unreason and the triumphant discovery of a new faculty. This sense is lost in the chaos of drugs, which gives contradictory dreams the semblance of profound intelligence."[5]

Lugné-Poë found that his stammer "made it difficult for him to get started." But he was "sensitive in the highest degree," and his characterization was excellent. "His makeup, his poses were those of an artist lost among actors."[6] He had a greater temperamental affinity with the next actor-manager he met, Charles Dullin, who, like Artaud, had once intended to be a priest. He was now running a theater, the Atelier, and a school for actors. After being taken on as a trainee, Artaud wrote in October 1921 to Yvonne Gilles, a young painter whom he'd met at a hospital in 1917, "All the action takes place in the soul." Having to improvise in class, the actor was told not to represent his spiritual movements but to *think* them. The purpose of Dullin's principles of instruction was "to *internalize* the actor's performance."[7] Long before Cheryl Crawford, Elia Kazan, and Robert Lewis founded The Actors Studio in New York, Dullin—often joining in the exercises he devised—made his students impersonate a wind, a fire, or a vegetable, sometimes a dream or a mental event.

Falling in love with a Romanian actress, Génica Athanasiou, Artaud struggled against his bondage to opium. In an early poem he called St. Francis of Assisi "that eternal absent from himself," which also described Artaud, but it felt as if Génica were never absent from him.[8] August Strindberg, at the start of his relationship with the actress Harriet Bosse, who became his third wife, had the same illusion about being with her when he wasn't.

In a letter written during the summer of 1922, Artaud declared that art was the *double* of life, a duplicate reality. "We have a spirit so made that

4
Hayman, *Artaud and After*, 37.

5
O.C. 1, bk. 2, 52–54.

6
A.-M. Lugné-Poë, article in *L'Éclair*, 18 December 1932.

7
Selected Writings, 17.

8
Selected Writings, 4.

it spends its life looking for itself . . . In becoming conscious, it duplicates itself."[9] Writing verse and prose, acting and designing sets, he ventured defiantly away from realism. As an actor, he devised grotesque makeups, imitated animal behavior, distorted the sound of his voice, galvanized his frail body into convulsions that mingled his personal anguish with that of the character. He loved theater as a means of abolishing the gap between experience and audience, but hated the repetition involved in giving performances.

Blaming civilization for the fragmentation that stops us from enjoying what Maurice Maeterlinck called the "symbolic meaning of things, their secret transactions," he responded enthusiastically to literature and paintings such as Paul Klee's, which offer "cosmic syntheses in which all the secret objectivity of things is made tangible."[10] Artaud snatched formulations like this one out of increasing desperation. Struggling against illness, depression, drug addiction, and financial distress, he found each exacerbated the others. "My suffering is so intense," he told Génica in August 1924, "that my soul seems about to snap."[11] Uncertain how much of his self-pity was due to opium, she found the relationship almost unbearable.

Antonin Artaud (right) in The Passion of Joan of Arc *(1928), directed by Carl Dreyer.*

He was making his mark as both a movie actor and a Surrealist. His film career started in 1923 with a role in Claude Autant-Lara's short film *Fait-Divers*. Artaud's two best parts were Marat in Abel Gance's 1927 *Napoléon* (filmed in 1925–26) and Jean Massieu in Carl Dreyer's 1928 *The Passion of Joan of Arc*. He told an interviewer that the good film actor "does

9
Hayman, *Artaud and After*, 45.

10
Selected Writings, 27.

11
Hayman, *Artaud and After*, 51.

12
Selected Writings, 184–85.

13
Louis Aragon, *Une Vague de rêves* (privately printed, n.d.).

14
La Révolution Surréaliste, no. 2 (15 January 1925).

15
Hayman, *Artaud and After*, 56.

16
La Révolution Surréaliste, no. 3 (15 April 1925): 16–17.

something that no one else could do, something that he himself in his normal state does not do."[12] But he'd give up acting if a role made him feel cut off from his thoughts and feelings.

The self-confidence he'd acquired in movies helped him assert himself successfully after he joined the Surrealists in October 1924. On 10 November his photograph appeared in the first issue of *La Révolution Surréaliste*, which proclaimed: "We must formulate a new declaration of human rights." On January 23, 1925, he was put in charge of the Bureau Central de Récherches Surréalistes (Central Bureau for Surrealist Research), which had just opened in the Rue de Grenelle. Louis Aragon called it "a romantic inn for unclassifiable ideas and continuing revolts. All that still remained of hope in this despairing universe would turn its last, raving glances towards our pathetic stall."[13] That month, Artaud had published a tract defining Surrealism as "a means of totally liberating the spirit and everything that resembles it." Coupling the words "Surrealism" and "revolution" pointed, he went on, to the "disinterested, detached, and even quite desperate character of this revolution."[14] In a speech given in Madrid in April, Aragon said: "I announce the advent of a dictator. Antonin Artaud is the man who attacked the ocean . . . He will have respect for nothing—not your schools, your lives, or your most secret thoughts."[15]

Editing the third issue of *La Révolution Surréaliste*, Artaud wrote most of it himself. It announced the end of the Christian era, and in "Address to the Pope" he accused God of thinking up all evil. "From top to bottom of your Roman masquerade what triumphs is hatred of the soul's immediate truths." Turning to the Dalai Lama, Artaud prayed for illumination "in a language our contaminated European minds can understand."[16]

Some of the Surrealists' revolutionary work was published by the conservative Éditions de la Nouvelle Revue Française, who brought out Artaud's *Umbilicus of Limbo* in 1925. Seventy years later, readers might be reminded of Samuel Beckett: "Leave your tongue, Paolo Uccello, leave your tongue, my tongue, my tongue, shit, who is speaking, where are you? Beyond, beyond, Mind,

Mind, fire, tongues of fire, fire, fire, eat your tongue, old dog, eat his tongue, eats, etc. I tear out my tongue."[17] But of course it's Beckett who's reminiscent of Artaud. The nineteen-fifties prose that curls back on itself, like a tongue exploring its roots, makes a point like the one Artaud made in 1946: "In my unconscious it's always other people that I hear."[18] Throughout his life he struggled to free himself from the common stock of phrases to attain the purity of independent existence. The two main differences between the thirty-year-old Surrealist and the fifty-year-old madman were that the older man had to manage without the support of a group and, partly for that reason, became more nihilistic. In a 1947 letter to the Surrealists' former leader, André Breton, Artaud said society no longer understood any language "except bombs, machine guns, barricades, and everything else that follows."[19] The prose poems he wrote before he broke with the Surrealists in November 1926 suggest that disruption of the rationalistic network of relationships can "provide access to death, put us in touch with . . . more refined states of mind."[20] And in "Letter to the Clairvoyant," the presence of the clairvoyant is reassuring, like opium. Opening doors into his brain cells, she makes it seem unnecessary to exert mental effort.[21]

In 1926, collaborating with the playwright Roger Vitrac, Artaud planned a theater to be named after Alfred Jarry, a precursor of Surrealism who died in 1907. Reacting against the "false and facile drama of the bourgeoisie,"[22] they wanted to ignore decor, costumes, and lighting, and abandon docile subservience to the script: "We must wait and seize the images that arise in us, naked, natural, excessive, and follow these images to the very end."[23] In the manifesto he published in *La Nouvelle Revue Française*, the tone was religious. "Our inability *to believe*, to accept illusion, is immense." The new theater would evolve productions with a profound sense that "an intimate part of our lives was involved in that spectacle."[24]

The austerity of his proposals had roots in the Catholic education he'd been given. The audience member should leave the theater in a state of "*human* anguish" after being "shaken and antago-

nized by the internal dynamic of the spectacle that will unfold before his eyes. . . . But a single miracle would be sufficient reward for our efforts and our patience. We count on this miracle."[25] He saw that "the Revolution most urgently needed consists of a kind of regression into time. Let us return to the mentality or even simply to the way of life of the Middle Ages."[26] Their first production was a triple bill including one-act plays by Artaud and Vitrac. "Our objective," Artaud wrote to Jean Paulhan in 1927, "has been to realize the soul's most secret movements through the simplest and barest means."[27] But his main commitment at this time was to the cinema. Instead of staging a second production, he played a monk in Dreyer's film, much of which was shot in closeups, and wrote a screenplay, *The Seashell and the Clergyman*, which was directed by Germaine Dulac. "The human skin of things," he said, "the epidermis of reality: this is the primary raw material of cinema. Cinema exalts matter and reveals it to us in its profound spirituality, in its relations with the spirit from which it has emerged."[28]

Towards the end of the year he became depressed. "My inner enthusiasm is dead," he told Dr. Allendy. "[T]here is something rotten in me."[29] But the Alfred Jarry Theater staged three more productions, including Vitrac's *Victor*, which had to be recast because the leading actress refused to play a woman who kept farting. In a program note Artaud explained that this represented moral grief and the poisoning of matter. As in the cinema, he wanted to articulate disturbance and desperation in physical terms; his prime concern was with what he thought of as inner spirit. Directing actors in the theater, he tried to approximate the language he thought ideal for the cinema—nonverbal and incapable of being translated into verbal terms. Inevitably, his interest in cinema began to dwindle as sound came in.

His "Theater of Cruelty" was inspired by non-Western theater, particularly from seeing Balinese dancers at the Colonial Exhibition in Paris in July 1931. Without words, the story was being told through "states of mind, which are themselves ossified and reduced to gestures—to

17
Selected Writings, 61.

18
Hayman, *Artaud and After*, 58.

19
Ibid.

20
Selected Writings, 124 n.

21
Selected Writings, 125–29.

22
"Le Théâtre de l'Atelier," *La Criée*, no. 17 (October 1922).

23
Selected Writings, 55.

24
Selected Writings, 155–56.

25
Selected Writings, 157–58.

26
Selected Writings, 162.

27
O.C. 3, 131.

28
Selected Writings, 151–52.

29
Selected Writings, 169.

structures."[30] The audience could reconcile external phenomena with its inner life. His quarrel with the bourgeois theater centered on its delineation of individual character and personal emotions, its discussion of psychological and social issues. He found that traditional theater had lost touch with the spirit of anarchy he considered essential to all poetry. But, unlike the Surrealists, he was turning back to Jewish mystics and early Christian writers. His idea of spirit was founded on essentialist and religious assumptions, while his distaste for contemporary culture and the scientific method was partly the cause and partly the result of his nostalgia for primitive and oriental cosmographies. He was thinking in terms of metaphysics and exorcism, magic and mysticism.

He conceived the phrase "Theater of Cruelty" as a name for a theater project when he had to withdraw a claim that he was going to run a Théâtre de la Nouvelle Revue Française, with a management committee including André Gide, Paul Valéry, and Paulhan, who'd succeeded Jacques Rivière as editor. To Paulhan he wrote, "Essentially cruelty means strictness, diligence, and implacable resolution, irreversible and absolute determination." In all practical cruelty there was "a sort of superior determinism to which the torturer-executioner is himself subject . . . Cruelty is above all lucid, a sort of rigorous discipline, submission to necessity." It is consciousness that "gives to every act of living its blood-red tinge, its hint of cruelty, because it's clear that life is always the death of someone else."[31] His formulations, he told Gide, were intended to inaugurate a new theatrical era in which "the director becomes the author, that is, the creator." He wanted to "create a physical and spatial poetry that has long been lacking in the theater."[32] He promised that productions would include work by Sade and Elizabethan plays stripped of their dialogue. Only characters, costumes, and situations would be kept. He proposed, unrealistically, that Western speech be jettisoned in favor of oriental incantation. In the first Theater of Cruelty manifesto he insisted that the new theatrical language must utilize "the nervous magnetism of man, to transgress the ordinary limits of art and speech, in order to

30
Selected Writings, 215.

33
Selected Writings, 245.

34
Anaïs Nin, The Journals of Anaïs Nin, ed. Gunther Stuhlmann (London: Calder, 1966).

35
Ibid.

31
O.C. 4, 121.

32
Selected Writings, 299, 301.

36
Hayman, Artaud and After, 93.

realize actively, that is magically, *in real terms*, a kind of total creation, in which man can only resume his place between dreams and events."[33] His aim was to exploit "all the slips of the mind and the tongue, which reveal what might be called the impotences of speech." Now, as so often, preoccupation with his personal debility dictated the terms of his program for revolution.

He was at the height of his powers when the cumulative effect of the drugs unbalanced him. Attracted by the idea that the plague liquefies all social structures, he lectured at the Sorbonne in April 1933 on "Theater and Plague." Anaïs Nin described in her diary how he screamed deliriously as his argument disintegrated into crazy acting. Demonstrating what it was like to be a victim of the plague, he drew on his own desperation. Embarrassed, the audience laughed, jeered, hissed. People walked out, leaving him writhing on the floor. Walking through the dark streets with her afterwards, he said that instead of just talking about the plague, he'd wanted to give people the experience itself, "so they'll be terrified and wake up. I want to wake them up."[34] Two months later, when he asked whether he was mad, she decided "that he was, and that I loved his madness. I looked at his mouth, with the edges darkened by laudanum, a mouth I didn't want to kiss. To be kissed by Artaud was to be drawn towards death, towards insanity." He was impatient for a revolution, "a catastrophe, a disaster that would put an end to his intolerable life."[35]

In 1933 he wrote the second manifesto for the Theater of Cruelty and a text, "An End to Masterpieces," calling for a new theater that would subordinate human psychology to historical necessity. Theatrical performance could connect microcosm and macrocosm, mental imbalance and public chaos. "I think there's a human duty to take account of all the evil forces that constitute the Zeitgeist," he wrote Orane Demazis in December 1933. "There's somewhere a disordering we can't control . . . All sorts of inexplicable crimes inside the self, gratuitous crimes, are part of this disordering. So are the far too frequent occurrences of earthquakes, volcanic eruptions, marine tornados, and railway accidents."[36] The word "disordering" (*dérèglement*) was the word the sixteen-year-old Rimbaud had used over sixty years earlier when he claimed drugs were helping him to penetrate the unknown. "The poet makes himself into a visionary by means of a long, immense, and calculated disordering of all the senses."[37] If Artaud was following a similarly painful path, it wasn't because he'd chosen to. Drugs intended to alleviate his sufferings were weakening his ability to distinguish between internal and external events, making him believe he could find "an analogy between a gesture made in painting or the theater and a gesture made by lava in a volcanic eruption."[38] Surrealism had given him a solidarity with other anarchic eccentrics, but now, having become more isolated, he was verging on madness.

He'd expected help from Paulhan in raising funds for the new theater. When this wasn't forthcoming, he withdrew the essay "The Alchemical Theater," which he'd offered to the *N.R.F.*, and launched a private appeal to prospective backers by giving a one-man reading of Shakespeare's *Richard II* in the house of a potential patron, Lise Deharme. The evening was a fiasco, but he was more successful with another fund-raising event, at the house of his friend Jean-Marie Conty in January 1934, when Artaud read his adaptation of Percy Bysshe Shelley's 1819 play *The Cenci*. The guests included two would-be actresses, Cécile Brassant, who was married to the publisher Robert Denoël, and Iya Abdy, a beautiful blonde of Russian origin. By promising parts to both women, Artaud raised the money he needed.

The Cenci is about the murder of an incestuous sixteenth-century count by his daughter. Artaud's interest in incest was based partly on the belief that it could precipitate a revelation of "cosmic cruelty." The "tempestuous" passions of Shelley's characters raised them above ordinary humanity. In his dying moment, the count predicts the supremacy of evil on earth; striking a Sadean note, Artaud makes him blame God for giving him an irresistibly desirable daughter, and generalize his sinfulness by saying there's "something like a devil inside me, destined to avenge the world's transgressions." Sharing this

37
Arthur Rimbaud to Paul Demeny, 15 May 1871, Rimbaud, *Oeuvres complètes* (Paris: Gallimard, 1972), 251.

38
Selected Writings, 257.

39
Selected Writings, 341.

40
André Franck, preface to *Lettres d'Antonin Artaud à Jean-Louis Barrault* (Paris: Bordas, 1952).

41
Hayman, *Artaud and After*, 98.

viewpoint, his daughter, Beatrice, complains that no moral choice has been made by God or man or "any of the powers that control what is called our destiny." She justifies her amorality by linking it with that of thunderstorms, hurricanes, and floods. "I . . . attack order itself," Artaud told Gide. "I strike hard to strike fast, but above all to strike completely and without possibility of appeal."[39]

Artaud, who both directed and played the count, had difficulty in explaining his ideas to the actors, and quarrelled with Iya Abdy. Having provided most of the backing, she felt disinclined to obey orders, and she didn't trust him. Wanting it to look as though she were hanging by her magnificent blonde hair from the torturer's wheel, he arranged for her to stand on a stool that was hidden from the audience. Afraid that he was going to kick the stool from under her feet on the first night to make her reaction more truthful, she infuriated him by refusing to be hanged.[40]

Commercially disastrous though the production was, it was influential. Michel Leiris has described how the objectivizing of collective delirium cut across traditional techniques,[41] and in many ways it prefigured the 1964 production of *Marat/Sade* by the most Artaudian of contemporary directors, Peter Brook. Trying to make his actors think of themselves as rapacious men of the Renaissance, Artaud used what he'd learnt from Dullin, telling each actor, for example, to choose an animal image for himself. Roger Blin, who, like Artaud, suffered from a stammer, and who was later to work with both Genet and Beckett, made his debut in a silent part—one of the assassins. "You're a medium," Artaud said. "Make your face up in four quarters, two green, two red." Like the whole production, many of the other makeups were stylized. One face was gray all over.

This was the last production Artaud directed. After watching Jean-Louis Barrault's mime of a horse in *Autour d'une mère*, which was based on Faulkner's *As I Lay Dying*, he waited for the young actor, who later wrote: "The two of us went down the boulevard Rochechouart, and together we started off on two imaginary horses, galloping as far as the Place Blanche. Then he suddenly left me. He was drunk with enthusiasm."[42] Reviewing the production, he saluted a younger man endowed with the ability to please the public. The show had magic in it, Artaud said, like the magic of black witch doctors who drive out disease by simulating the sick man's breathing. Barrault's mime demonstrated the importance of gesture and movement, the nonverbal expressiveness of the actor's body. He compared Barrault with Balinese dancers, awarding the accolade he had hoped to win. Through Barrault, Artaud exerted more influence on French theater than he had through his own activity in it. The two men used to meet almost every day. He introduced Barrault to Tantric Yoga, Hatha Yoga, the Tibetan Book of the Dead, the Upanishads, and the Bhagavad Gita. He talked about magic and metaphysics. He taught Barrault about the Cabala, which divides human breathing into six main "arcana," each involving a different combination of masculine, feminine, and neuter. As in acupuncture, said Artaud, there are pressure points in the body which support physical exertion and come into play when affective thought is emerging. The actor should agitate these pressure points as if whipping muscles into action.

Barrault exploited what he learnt: his theatrical activity was a stewing pot in which Artaud's ideas went on fermenting. His analogy between theater and the plague led to a dramatization, which Barrault commissioned, of Camus's novel *The Plague*. The resulting play, *The State of Siege*, was staged in October 1948, seven months after Artaud's death.

Barrault wanted to collaborate with Artaud, but collaboration involves compromise. He told Barrault in 1935: "I WON'T HAVE, in a spectacle staged by myself, so much as the flicker of an eye that does not belong to me."[43] Having failed to subdue his cast in *The Cenci*, he knew he was asking for the impossible, but drugs had exacerbated his obstinacy. As he put it in a letter to René Thomas ten months later, when he was already in Mexico and about to set out on a journey to the interior, "I'm leaving in search of the impossible. We'll see whether I can nevertheless find it."[44] He was still questing for a

theater of cruelty, but no longer hoping to create it in Paris. "I believe that in Mexico there are still seething forces that pressurize the blood of the Indians," he told Paulhan. "There the theater which I imagine, which perhaps I contain within myself, expresses itself directly, without the intervention of actors who can betray me."[45]

Since 1933 he'd been making notes on non-Western, Greek, and Indian cultures. Going to his hotel, wrote André Franck, one found him lying on his bed with the Upanishads or the Tibetan Book of the Dead.[46] He presumably had access to the library of Dr. Allendy, who'd been researching a book on the Black Death, but Artaud's bias was antimodern, antihumanist, anti-individualist, and antipsychological. "Squeeze a man hard and you'll always find something inhuman."[47] Hoping to find residue from the pre-Cortez civilization, he thought he could teach the Mexicans how theater could produce a rediscovery of culture. "Culture isn't in books, paintings, statues, dances: it's in the nerves and the fluidity of the nerves."[48] By August 1935 he was preparing lectures. "In Mexico, bound into the earth, lost in the flow of volcanic lava, vibrating in the Indian blood, there is the magic reality of a culture that could doubtless be materially ignited without much difficulty."[49] The dualistic rift between body and mind must be healed. If the gods of the ancient Mexican pantheon looked savage and primitive, it was because they hadn't had time to dehumanize themselves, and they'd never lost their potency because they were identical with active natural forces. The same month, after writing no verse for eight years, he began again. No longer believing actors could bridge the chasm between the outside world and the point at which his ideas began, he needed another outlet for his creativity.

He sailed from Antwerp on 10 January 1936, and within three weeks of his arrival in Mexico, he was lecturing at the University of Mexico on "Theater and the Gods." Since life is magical, and fire present in all manifestations of human thought, theater should display this element of thought that catches fire. Writing freezes the mind, but theater calls up the power of the gods, and in a series of newspaper articles he argued

42
Jean-Louis Barrault, *Memories for Tomorrow*, trans. J. Griffin (London: Thames and Hudson, 1974).

45
Ibid.

46
Franck, preface to *Lettres d'Antonin Artaud à Jean-Louis Barrault*.

47
O.C. 8, 144.

48
Hayman, *Artaud and After*, 101.

49
O.C. 8, 159.

43
Selected Writings, 343.

44
Hayman, *Artaud and After*, 101.

that Mexico was the only place where dormant natural forces could be helpful to the living. His plan was to revive pagan pantheism in a form that would no longer be religious.

Though he'd been making efforts to give up heroin, he was still taking it, and after his journey into the interior, Tarahumara Indians involved him in a ceremony at which goats were slaughtered and everyone was given grated peyote, or mescal-button, from which mescaline is derived. He became convinced that the Tarahumara had reunited the male and female principles and thought he'd learned something from them about attachment to an idea of the divine, together with detachment from the values and attitudes of society.

Returning to France in November 1936, he was penniless and ill, and in May 1937, lecturing in Brussels on his Mexican experiences, he lost control and insulted the audience. In the delirious pamphlet "New Revelations of Being," he insisted that he was no longer in the world and proposed to throw himself into the void. Believing a cane he'd been given had been used by Christ to fight against devils in the desert, and had afterwards belonged to St. Patrick, he went to Ireland in August, and had several brushes with the police before being deported to France. He apparently attacked two mechanics on the ship and had to be forcibly restrained. He arrived in a straitjacket and in October was interned in a psychiatric hospital in Rouen. In April 1938 he was moved to the asylum of Sainte-Anne in Paris; in 1939 to Ville-Évrard in the suburbs of Paris. He was moved again in January 1943 to the asylum at Rodez, where the medical director, Dr. Gaston Ferdière, found the most effective therapy for him, aside from electroshock treatment, was through art. He'd done no drawing or painting since designing for Dullin in the twenties, but he responded positively when Ferdière praised his drawings and when Frédéric Delanglade, a local painter, took him to his studio. He drew a charcoal portrait of Delanglade, "rubbed it out, began another and repeated this process several times."[50]

In March 1946, after spending over eight consecutive years in asylums, he was released

50
Tour de feu
(Bordeaux),
nos. 63–64.

from Rodez, six months before his fiftieth birthday. He'd been persuaded to stay at a clinic in Ivry. Having started drawing and painting in Rodez, he went on after being discharged.

He was to make one last attempt at a theatrical performance. On 13 January 1947, when he appeared at the Vieux Colombier, Gide, Barrault, and Camus were among the three hundred people in the audience. He declaimed three poems, almost inaudibly, sobbing and stammering, before trying to describe his experiences in Ireland and Mexico. He talked about the electric shock treatments he'd been given at Rodez and about black magic. He read another poem, improvised, broke off. According to some reports he went on roaring and shouting abuse until his voice gave out; according to others he ran from the stage in terror. Gide afterwards described "his big ungainly figure, his face consumed by inner fire, his hands that knot themselves together either held out towards unreachable help or twisting in anguish. More often tightly shielding his face, alternately hiding and revealing it, openly signalling abominable human distress, a sort of unreprievable damnation, with no escape, except into a frantic lyricism, nothing of which could reach the audience except scatological flashes, curses, and blasphemies."[51]

51
André Gide,
"Antonin Artaud,"
Combat, 19
March 1948: 6.

Three weeks later he visited the van Gogh exhibition at the Orangerie. "I am also like poor van Gogh. I no longer think, but each day I come closer to the explosions I'm producing . . . Van Gogh has seized the moment when the pupil of the eye is going to spill into the void . . . what is more, nothingness has never harmed anybody, but what pushes me back inside myself is this desolating absence which passes and momentarily submerges me, but I see there clearly, very clearly. I even know what nothingness is, and I'll be able to say what there is inside it."[52] He'd been complaining, increasingly, of intestinal pain. He was suffering from an inoperable cancer, and at the clinic on 4 March, the caretaker who was bringing his breakfast found him dead.

52
Selected Writings,
509–10.

"I am the body's insurgent . . ."
Marthe Robert

The old cliché of the curse said to afflict certain poets, as though their misfortune had no causes other than this decree placed on them somehow by someone, finds a semblance of life when considering Antonin Artaud's destiny. In trying to grasp the poignant face of a man who was and who wanted to be indefinable, it is tempting to fall back on this image, for lack of something better, but it no longer suffices. For what made Artaud's life an existence of perpetual torture, and even now creates an abnormal posthumous situation by condemning to silence an essential part of his work, is not a curse proceeding from some vague, unknowable fate; it is something that has a name and is precisely that which all of Artaud's work despairingly denounces. For us, Artaud is not the last of the *poètes maudits*, but rather the first to have rebelled totally, cease-lessly, against all that tries, in complicity with thought and words, to enclose within acceptable limits the strange, ever new, intolerable scandal of suffering. This insurrection that overcomes its own limits—for it, like suffering, is limitless, endless, and without purpose—is the very pulse of Artaud's life, the sole source of his inspiration, the beginning and end of his work.

Should we say that Artaud wrote because he was rebelling and that he rebelled because he suffered? Is the path so short from real suffering to the "general throes of denial" to which the tortured poet ultimately reduced all poetry? As simple as it may seem, suffering is nevertheless the only explanation that does not let us forget the essential thing: that the sickness of Antonin Artaud, this existence-sickness, this sickness of being, which he would one day cease to describe in order to shout it at the top of his lungs, is essentially an inhuman condition from which there is no way out. Artaud's work is not an *oeuvre* but the desperate search for an exit; it revolves entirely around a cry of suffering; it is the cry itself, neither beautiful, nor harmonious, nor pathetic, but simply true.

"Poet enraged by truth," the beautiful name he gave the "unthinkable Comte de Lautréamont," is probably the only one he would have claimed for himself. This rage was in fact his own; he was able to speak because of this rage, which corresponds to "all the rages of existence-sickness," to say outright who he was,

Antonin Artaud, 1937.

to name the suffering that made him a man apart, separated for some incomprehensible reason not only from others but from life. Upon his entrance into Letters through the narrow door of the "sacrosanct N. R. F. [*Nouvelle Revue Française*]," he wrote to [its editor] Jacques Rivière, less for the purpose of showing his poems to him than to reveal himself; and it is clear that he was not driven by banal sincerity, even less by a juvenile desire to attract attention, but by the urgent need to be accepted as he was, the sole proof of his worth being the enormous weight of his singularity. As a man who had always suffered, not only from his own pain but from society's attitude toward him, Artaud informed the world—in this case, the severe but

ultimately well-meaning critic of his poems—
that the illness with which he was afflicted was a
"genuine sickness," something that should be
neither excused, forgotten, attenuated, isolated,
nor judged, but entirely accepted as part of him.

Thus he asserted that his poems' shortcomings
were hardly ordinary flaws due to a lack of
practice or a novice's awkwardness, but that they
were closely linked to his sickness, which is
not "a phenomenon of the age" but "a sickness
which touches the essence of being and its
central possibilities of expression, and which
applies itself to a whole life." And so as not to risk
being misunderstood, he tracked down on
all sides what continually distanced him from
himself and mutilated his inner being. It was,
he said, "a central collapse of the soul . . . a
kind of erosion, both essential and fleeting, of
thought . . . a temporary nonpossession of the
material benefits of my development . . . an
abnormal separation of the elements of
thought." Barely had he described the condition
that prevented him from fully and totally
communicating what he had to say—and which
he evoked with a rare felicity of expression, as
Jacques Rivière noted, not without some irony—
when he added this sentence, laying bare the very
root of his revolt: "So trust me." And later: "One
must not be too quick to judge men, one must
trust them to the point of absurdity, to the dregs."
Such a call for unconditional trust, beyond all
judgment and all proof, is here again a plea.
Later, after Artaud experienced the sort of trust
society was capable of giving him, the call would
be drowned by invective and shouting. If he
then turned toward fury, if he resolved himself
to absolute negation, it was because the only
response he ever got was silence, childish
appeasements, or a denial of trust that, one fine
day, brutally changed into aggression.

Shortly before his death, Artaud wrote: "Make
room for the young, the newcomers, in place of
those who have nothing more to say, but who are
here. The place stinks. But it still doesn't stink
enough to ward off criticism, or attack, or
judgment, or aggression of whatever nature
against me. And does it matter to me? In reality,
I could remain indifferent and I could stay above

it and scorn it, but the unfortunate thing is that
it does matter to me." For someone who cannot
"stay above it," criticism, attack, and judgment
are one and the same. Well-meaning or hostile,
tacit or spoken, inscribed in law, science, or
reason, the judgment of others, of all others,
whether they are dead or alive, whether they
speak from a distance or remain silent, was for
Artaud the worst insult to suffering, a true
violation of life. This is why, in his work, from
beginning to end, he hunted down thought that
was set up as judge; his whole quest was to find a
weapon capable of destroying this single enemy.

Judgment is all the more dangerous in that its
effects are insidious and elusive. We see this in
Rivière's responses, though his good will cannot
be doubted. Clearly, the critic was in an awkward
position: what does one say to a man who puts so
much passion and talent into declaring himself
incapable of everything, of thought and literature as well as life? Instinctively, Rivière got himself out of the situation by using a common tactic;
he generalized the all-too-singular nature of the
case. In this, he unknowingly played the role of
all those who, in the immediate circle of the sick
child, then of the tormented adolescent, no doubt
attempted to deny the importance of his illness,
as much to appease his suffering as to relieve
themselves of an intolerable responsibility. "You
always exaggerate, you only suffer because you
think too much about it, calm down, you're not
the only one in this situation, everyone suffers,
etc." One can imagine how Artaud took these
arguments, which parents and teachers use in an
attempt to break the rebellion of every sensitive
child. At bottom, Rivière doesn't say anything
else. To this fundamental state, which Artaud
presented as unique and incomparable, Rivière
contrasted the malady of the epoch, the malaise
of contemporary literature, and more generally,
the impossibility of all thought to account for
itself absolutely. Through this, he very simply
cancelled out the singularity that bothered him,
and that was indeed bothersome, since no
recourse to generalization ever manages to abolish
it. By publishing these letters, Rivière did finally
find the only way to respond, at least in part, to
what had been asked of him. And yet, beneath

the critic's indulgent and somewhat paternal tone, Artaud could not help but feel once again the knife that always reopened his wound: he had been heard in a way, but not acknowledged.

Among all those who approached Artaud, who loved and admired him as a man and as a poet, how many can be sure of not having aggravated his suffering with a look, a question, a doubt? How many guessed that their advice, their appeasements, their words of consolation, indeed the way they remained silent at times, were for the perpetually guarded poet an intervention scarcely less scandalous than the coercive measures which society was legally able to use against him? We know this now: Artaud was right in refusing to distinguish among his judges; he knew that if trust were not accorded him absolutely, *to the point of absurdity, to the dregs,* the most seemingly inoffensive word could at any moment turn against him and condemn him. And we have seen, in fact, that faced with the singularity of suffering that can neither be explained satisfactorily, nor reduced or expelled, society gives only two replies: polite denial— no, no, you're like everyone else, don't think about it anymore, relax—or, alleging danger to the sufferer or to others, brutal annihilation. In both cases, the result is the same: whether it is benevolent or violent, whether it takes the form of friendly advice or a doctor's diagnosis, the negation of singularity entails for the being who is subjected to it the loss of what he has that is most authentic; in a true sense, it already is a death sentence.

How does one block out judgment that permeates life and stealthily contaminates it? First by unmasking all thought that, in the name of so-called knowledge, takes apart, separates, compares, analyzes, and ultimately confuses *discrimination* with the right to *incriminate*. The judgment of man by man is in fact based only on the unanimously recognized power of reason and its laws: therefore one must attack rational, logical thought in order to eliminate the seeds of iniquity contained in all judgment.

The spontaneous nature of his revolt united Artaud with a number of other minds that, at precisely this period, rose up with all the violence they were capable of against the pretensions of reason to say everything about man. But if he joined those who struggled, as he did, against rationalism in order to recapture real unity of thought, even if the shouts of his voice clearly dominated the clamor of the first Surrealist manifestos, he did not follow his companions for long, and the little ride he took with them soon left him more alone than ever. His reasons for struggling were not theirs, and, though he strongly desired the warmth of common battle, he could only fight as a *franc-tireur* for a goal that he alone saw. Here again, suffering separated him from the very people who were most like him and who, in the best of cases, only had a passing, fragmentary, intellectual experience of what he endured at every instant, not only mentally but physically. Artaud was quite aware of the source of the misunderstanding that would ultimately break out. "But they," he said to Rivière, speaking of poets who at the time were still his friends, "their soul is not physiologically damaged, not in its substance, it is damaged at all the points where it is connected with something else, it is not damaged outside of thought." And returning to the brutal fact that prohibited all comparison and all connection between him and the others: "The fact remains that they do not suffer and that I do suffer, not only in the mind but in the flesh and in my everyday soul. This lack of connection to the object that characterizes all of literature is in me a lack of connection to life." Excluded from the Surrealist movement by the very nature of the revolt that had brought him to it, Artaud must have found in this brief adventure the confirmation of his irremediable isolation: others could speak poetically of the absurd, the irrational, the permanent rebellion; he alone was forced to believe in it and actually conform his life to it.

Just as Artaud could not see in Surrealism an end in itself—for the surreal mattered much less to him than the real, from which he was separated[1]—he likewise found in the spiritual conceptions that attracted him only vague promises of salvation, something that could console, perhaps, but not radically change life. For a long time, certainly, he would assert the

[1] "For reality is frighteningly superior to all fiction, all fable, all divinity, all surreality. All you need is the genius of knowing how to interpret it." (*Van Gogh, the Man Suicided by Society,* 1947)

superiority of the East over the West, of "tradition" over logical thought, of total knowledge over analytical science, which is its mere caricature. He would also believe in myths, in all myths, in occult knowledge which once formed the science and wisdom of the West, in the forgotten truths of the most archaic civilizations. But all this was still an elsewhere and a beyond; all this had to do with a world where reconciliation was imagined without ever actually happening. Artaud could no longer wait for a beyond and an elsewhere; in order to live, he needed the world to change, instituting what he would later admirably call "a high measure of equity without secrecy."[2] He would one day go in geographic search of this true world, which no idea could replace, and seek its revelation among the remote Tarahumara. But from the very beginning, he sensed he would not find it except by creating it himself in the only domain in which he was permitted to act: on the stage of a theater.

"Every being has chanted a theater," wrote Artaud. "The universe is a theater." Because of its profound resemblance to the world, theater became for him an immediate kingdom of "absolute freedom in revolt," and he did not want to await its reign. To use this freedom regardless of the rules that here represent the very illusion of the law, to make a performance an act of insurrection and rigor, to outfit life in the most garish fashion in order to force it to show itself as it really is, to recapture a language that existed before value judgments froze the word—such was the task Artaud entrusted to theater, not in order to reform it, not to give it esthetic justification, but to convey in a visible representation at least part of the truth. If the Theater of Cruelty only had a brief existence, even if Artaud was its only author and its only actor, one can still say that the poet carried out his agenda to the dot, by confusing it with the very task of his life. (We cannot resist mentioning a poet here who could join the only family Artaud ever tolerated: that of his brothers through misery and genius. I do not remember hearing him speak of Kleist, but doubtless had Artaud known some of his plays— I am thinking in particular of *The Family Schroffenstein* and *Robert Guiskard*—he would

2
The whole passage must be quoted here:
Where does happiness come from sadness,
    joy?
From a high measure of equity without secrecy
    No one has ever possessed it
    No one has ever reached it
        Revolt took place.

have given them a place in the Theater of Cruelty's program. Von Kleist says nothing in his plays if not the "And so trust me" by which Artaud demands to be acknowledged. He, too, suffers from the feeling of being a "perpetual stammering cripple" and harbors a suspicion in regard to language that provides him with the real subject of his dramas. Finally, his relations with the Romantic movement are not unlike Artaud's with Surrealism. Just as Artaud seems to embody the ideal Surrealist hero, Kleist appears to be the true hero of a book that the Romantics did not write.)

Need we now point out that the ideas contained in *The Theater and Its Double*, despite the immense influence they had and still have on contemporary dramatic art, do not constitute, strictly speaking, a theory? Far less than a reflection on the theater, they are the expression of a revolt forced by its very origins to violently unmask appearances. The emphasis placed on cruelty and the physical necessities of the stage, the refusal of a psychology that casts feelings and passions in a language too clear to be true, the displacement of various elements of the performance, the substitution of incantation for futile "analyses of the word"—all this does not respond to the necessities of an esthetic system, but to the urgent need of a mind rebelling against everything that limits it, primarily against language, which most often elucidates and judges, instead of making words explode in the rage of truth.

The primary object of *The Theater and Its Double* is this truth, which, situated before language, must circulate not from mind to mind, but from body to body. As Artaud said, "in the state of degeneration we are in, it is through the skin that the metaphysical will re-enter the mind." Later, after the terrible crisis that almost separated him forever from the rest of mankind, Artaud would completely identify truth with the body, and from then on, it was in the name of this body alone—"nothing but the body such as we see it"—that he would ceaselessly rebel.

We know the last works of Artaud are no longer poems; they have to be heard as the cries of an illiterate rediscovering his mystery, "without alpha and without omega, but with a head, two legs, two arms." Finally, to do justice to this "hopeless illiterate simpleton who is man and does not understand," Artaud can only cry out by drawing up at length, with a patience burned through with rage, the catalogue of "dirty negations that become more and more remote," which destroy all ideas in order to prepare for the advent of the body—a body with neither alibi nor justification, with no equivalent in the mind, neither sanctified nor renewed by suffering, but bursting with horror to its limits, gaping with horror through all its openings, rising up against everything that still comes into it. It is the unintelligible "tumulus of flesh," which thought no longer has the right to touch. Amid the din that accompanies the collapse of ideas, notions, concepts, principles, definitions, the body alone remains standing, before or beyond value or quality. "Abolish values" and "no principles"— Artaud's last texts obstinately revolve around these rallying cries, which command him to annihilate all constructions by which thought has excluded itself from the order of life.

Pursued with total rigor, Artaud's revolt traverses all degrees of negation in order finally to come up against its principal obstacle: language, which is his primary tool and the last object that remains to be destroyed. Before attacking the enemy head on, this revolt begins by challenging what is most fragile about it: language is not what it pretends to be; it does not express but betrays; its betrayal consists precisely in its claim to elucidate everything, when in fact "true expression hides what it manifests." And each time language wants to utter the truth, it is false. It can only fulfill its highest function by becoming image, allegory, figure of speech— that is, poetic language.

As a "poet enraged by truth," however, Artaud soon discovers the impasse poetry reaches as soon as it is no longer ruled by the demands of Beauty alone. If poetry must hunt down ideas everywhere, it cannot spare the words that bear them. But to destroy the words is to condemn poetry to silence, and poetry cannot do this, since it must somehow communicate its revolt. Caught in the insoluble situation it has created for itself,

Artaud's poetry consents to its own destruction, but it annihilates itself with an instrument that it forged for itself first in order to provoke "this elipeptoid trepidation of the Word" that announces its apocalypse.

Paradoxically, it was in the period when he wrote the most that Artaud affirmed and repeated that he did not believe "in words or ideas stirred up by words and in words." No doubt, then, he wrote not only against words but against himself, against the love of language— of good-looking French, he said—that in fact had never left him and secretly opposed his revolt. At the time he wrote the pages that seemed to him to have been dictated—as if there were on his part neither choice, nor search, nor effort— he noted: "Style horrifies me, and I realize that when I write I always have some, so I burn all my manuscripts and I only keep those that remind me of a suffocation, a panting, a strangulation in some unknown dregs, because that is what is true." And again: "Therefore I see that for the thirty years I have been writing—I haven't quite found—not my words or my tongue—but the instrument I have never stopped forging." This instrument does not owe its strength to inspiration alone, as we would be tempted to believe, any more than its strange and tormented form can be explained by sickness. It is a work implement, a tool, a weapon, on which all the pain of the worker may still be seen.

Certainly Artaud is not the only poet to have had the dream of total revolt against what is, but no one has hurled so far and so high the "no" he said to the world at every moment. To say yes to things, to nature, to tenderness and love, he first needed to confirm "the high measure of equity without secrecy" without which suffering remains a suspicious hole where life itself is vilified. Refusing ever to surrender to the necessity of things as they are and the world as it is, Artaud wrote until the last moment "to have done with the Judgment of God." Through this, he also let us know that he wanted to have done with the judgment of men.

Translated by Jeanine Herman

Antonin Artaud : WORKS ON PAPER

50 Dessins pour assassiner la magie

ANTONIN ARTAUD : 31 JANUARY 1948

"50 Drawings to Assassinate Magic"

It's not a question here of
drawings
in the proper sense of the term,
of somehow incorporating
reality by drawing.
They are not an attempt
to renew
the art
in which I never believed
of drawing
no
but to understand them
you have first to situate them
These are 50 drawings
culled from various books
of notes
literary
poetic
psychological,
psychological
magical
especially magical
magical first
and foremost.
They are thus interwoven
into pages,
laid down on pages
where the writing
takes up the foreground of
vision,
writing,
the feverish note,
effervescent,
on fire
the blasphemy
the curse.

Il ne s'agit pas ici des
dessins
au propre sens du terme,
d'une incorporation quelconque
de la réalité par le dessin.
Ils ne sont pas une tentative
pour renouveler
l'art
auquel je n'ai jamais cru
du dessin
non
mais pour les comprendre
il faut les situer d'abord
Ce sont 50 dessins
pris a des cahiers
de notes
littéraires
poétiques
psychologiques,
psychologiques
magiques
magiques surtout
magiques d'abord
et par dessus tout.
Ils sont donc entremêlés
a des pages,
couchés sur des pages
où l'écriture
tient le 1er plan de
la vision,
l'écriture,
la note fièvreuse,
effervescente,
ardente
le blasphème
l'imprécation.

From curse to
curse
these pages
progress
and like new
sensitive
bodies
these drawings
are there
to provide commentary,
ventilation
and elucidation
These are not drawings
they figure nothing,
disfigure nothing,
are not there to
construct
edify
establish
a world
be it abstract

These are notes,
words,
shanks,
and being on fire
corrosive
incisive
spurted forth
from who knows what
vortex of
sub-maxillary,
sub-spatular
vitriol,
they are there as if
nailed in place
fated not to
make another move.
Mere shanks
but ready to carry out
their apocalypse
for they have spoken
too much of it to be born
and spoken too much in birth
not to be reborn
and
take on body
at last   authentically.

D'imprécation en
imprécations
ces pages
avancent
et comme des corps de
sensibilité
nouveaux
ces dessins
sont là
qui les commentent,
les aèrent
et les éclairent
Ce ne sont pas des dessins
ils ne figurent rien,
ne défigurent rien,
ne sont pas là pour
construire
édifier
instituer
un monde
même abstrait

Ce sont des notes,
des mots,
des trumeaux,
car ardents,
corrosifs
incisifs
jaillis
de je ne sais quel
tourbillon
de vitriol
sous maxillaire,
sous spatulaire,
ils sont là comme
cloués
et destinés à ne
plus bouger.
Trumeaux donc
mais qui feront
leur apocalypse
car ils en ont trop
dit pour naître
et trop dit en naissant
pour ne pas renaître
et
prendre corps
alors   authentiquement.

But all this
would be nothing
if one just had
to let it go at that,
not go beyond
the page
written
then illustrated
by the light
the flickerings
of these drawings
which mean nothing
and represent
absolutely nothing

To understand these drawings
as a whole
one has to
1) leave the written page
to enter into
the real
but
2) leave the real
to enter into
the surreal
the extra-real
the supernatural
the suprasensible
into which these drawings
keep on
plunging
seeing as they come from here
and seeing as they are in fact
but the commentary
on an action that
really took
place
and are but the circumscribed
figuration
on paper
of an élan
that took place
and produced
magnetically and
magically its
effects
and seeing as these
drawings are not the

Mais tout ceci
ne serait rien
si l'on devait
s'en tenir là,
ne pas sortir
de la page
écrite
puis illustrée
par la lumière
comme vacillante
de ces dessins
qui ne veulent rien dire
et ne représentent
absolument rien

Pour comprendre ces dessins
intégralement
il faut
1° sortir de la page écrite
pour entrer dans
le réel
mais
2° sortir du réel
pour entrer
dans le surréel,
l'extra-réel,
le surnaturel,
le suprasensible
où ces dessins
ne cessent
de plonger
parce qu'ils en viennent
et qu'ils ne sont en fait
que le commentaire
d'une action qui
a eu réellement
lieu,
que la figuration
sur le papier
circonscrite
d'un élan
qui a eu lieu
et a produit
magnétiquement et
magiquement ses
effets
et par ce qu'ils ne sont
pas ces dessins la

representation
or the
figuration
of an object
or a state of
mind or fear,
of a psychological
element
or event,
they are purely
and simply the
reproduction on
paper
of a magical
gesture
which I executed
in true space
with the breath of my
lungs
and my hands,
with my head
and 2 feet
with my trunk and my
arteries, etc.

When I write,
in general I just
dash down a
note
but this is not
enough for me
and I try to prolong
the action of what
I have written into
the atmosphere. So
I get up
I cast about
for consonances,
for adequations
of sound,
for swayings of the body
and limbs
as might constitute an act,
calling out
to the ambient spaces
to rise up
and speak
then I return

représentation
ou la
figuration
d'un objet
d'un état de
tête ou de peur,
d'un élément
et d'un événement
psychologique,
ils sont purement
et simplement la
reproduction sur le
papier
d'un geste
magique
que j'ai exercé
dans l'espace vrai
avec le souffle de mes
poumons
et mes mains,
avec ma tête
et mes 2 pieds
avec mon tronc et mes
artères etc,

Quand j'écris,
j'écris en général
une note d'un
trait
mais cela ne
me suffit pas
et je cherche à prolonger
l'action de ce que
j'ai écrit dans
l'atmosphère. Alors
je me lève
je cherche
des consonances,
des adéquations
de sons,
des balancements du corps
et des membres
qui fassent acte,
qui appellent
les espaces ambiants
à se soulever
et parler
puis je me rapproche

to the written
page
and . . .

But I forgot   to
say that these
consonances
have a sense,
I breathe, I sing,
I modulate
but not at random
no

I always have
some prodigious thing
or world
to create or call forth.

And I know
the plastic objective
value of breath,
breath is some
thing in the air
it is not just air
stirred
up.
It's a massive
concretisation in
the air
and which must
be felt
in the body and
by the body
like an atomic
agglomeration in short
of elements
and members
which at that moment
make up a table
a matter
far beyond
that of barley
sugar
is born at that
very moment
instantaneously
in the body,

de la page
écrite
et . . .

Mais j'oubliais   de
dire que ces
consonances
ont un sens,
je souffle, je chante,
je module
mais pas au hasard
non

J'ai toujours
comme un objet prodigieux
ou un monde
à créer et à appeler.

Or je connais
la valeur plastique
objective du souffle,
le souffle c'est quelque
chose dans l'air
ce n'est pas de l'air
remué
seulement.
C'est une concrétisation
massive dans
l'air
et qui doit
être sentie
dans le corps et
par le corps
comme une agglomération
en somme atomique
d'éléments
et de membres
qui à ce moment là
font tableau
une matière
très au delà
de celle du sucre
d'orge
nait à ce moment
là
instantanément
dans le corps,

Electri-
cal matter
which might
explain
if it were
itself
explicable
the nature
of certain
atomic gasses
of certain
repellent atoms

I say atoms
as I would say
bare wall,
volcanic rock face,
a volcano's artery
in fusion,
wall of lava
marching towards
a reversal of
the immediate   becoming,

my drawings hence reproduce
these forms
thus evident,
these worlds of
marvels,
these objects
where the Way
is made
and that which
one called in alchemy
the Great Work henceforth
was pulverized, for we
are no longer in
chemistry
but in
nature
and I firmly believe
that
nature
shall speak

Translated by Richard Sieburth

Matière électri-
que
qui pourrait
expliquer
si elle était
elle même
explicable
la nature
de certains gaz
atomiques
de certains
atomes répulsifs

Je dis atomes
comme je dirai
pan de mur,
paroi volcanique,
artère en fusion d'un
volcan,
muraille de lave en
marche vers un
renversement de
l'immédiat   devenir,

mes dessins donc reproduisent
ces formes
ainsi apparues,
ces mondes de
prodiges,
ces objets
où la Voie
est faite
et ce qu'on
appelait le grand oeuvre
alchimique désormais
pulvérisé, car nous ne
sommes plus dans
la chimie
mais dans la
nature
et je crois bien
que la
nature
va parler

I. Spells and Gris-Gris

1937–1944

*Envelope of letter from Artaud
to André Breton, 1937*

Agnès de la Beaumelle

Strange little pieces of paper, written and drawn upon, often stained and burned, bearing imprecations, the "spells" issued by Antonin Artaud beginning in September 1937, sent from Dublin, Sainte-Anne Hospital, and the Ville-Évrard asylum, are integral parts of written letters and thus constitute, aside from an exercise in magic, actual missives. That the epistolary terrain should be chosen for the resumption—or, rather, reinvention—of graphic activity, more than ten years after he had apparently given up drawing for the theater, should not be surprising from someone who, starting in 1924 with the letters to Jacques Rivière, the "addresses" to the Pope and the Dalai Lama, to the Rectors of the European Universities and the Head Doctors of the Insane Asylums, and so forth, established his writing as a demonstrative act, defensive and offensive, sent to another as a gesture of protest. Out of the disastrous experience in Ireland, out of the despair of confinement in asylums, the need to multiply invectives and appeals would be developed in a mode yet more "barbarous" with the spells. The urgency of literally emitting "signs" of life, of sending tangible messages whose significance had to be perceived by the recipient right away, whose effectiveness had to be immediate, led him to find a totally new means of graphic expression. In many ways, these imprecatory letters, drawn upon and often violently colored, functioning magically, can be considered explosive attacks that inaugurate the unique method of drawing—in terms of function and status—practiced by Artaud starting in 1945 at Rodez, then at Ivry, a close suburb of Paris. "I had made up my mind," he would write in 1947, "to *coax out* those forms, lines, outlines, shadows, colors . . . which would create, as it were, above the paper a kind of counter-figure which would be an ongoing protest against the laws of the

created object." Here the function of exorcism and insurrection is announced, to which all the later "awkward" drawings—"counter-figures" to use his term—correspond; here the necessity of an act of total *ex*pression is defined, where writing and drawing, the physical and oral, function together. Messages, testimonies, incantations, imprecations—such would be the large sheets of Rodez, as well as the portraits of the last period filled with glossolalia or graphic expulsions.

More precisely, in 1937, the spells constitute proofs, notionally operative, of the magic power foreshadowed when, upon returning from Mexico, Artaud had called himself "Le Révélé" (The Revealed), and when, armed with Saint Patrick's cane, he went like a shaman to reveal to the Irish their lost secrets. Though sometimes charged with protective powers, the spells generally emit forces of death or vengeance, threats against everything that from that time forward seemed "impure" to Artaud: sexual practices, alliances with money and power, the contempt of God. The recipients of these unsettling missives varied: the spells that we know of (Paule Thévenin has catalogued seven, but one may suppose that many disappeared, that they were lost, or that the hospital administration had them confiscated, or even that those in possession of them were too attached to them to disclose them) are addressed to close friends (Roger Blin), most often women (Lise Deharme, Sonia Mossé, Jacqueline Breton), or to doctors (Dr. Fouks, Dr. Lubtchansky), and, very rarely, to public figures (Hitler)—recipients on whom they were supposed to act *physically*.

The first ones, sent from Dublin, retain the appearance of letters: the violence of the words that pour forth overshadows the drawn elements; the page is still usually filled with written lines, interrupted only by a few cabalistic figures or marks (those of his signature, the date), traces or holes burnt by a cigarette, or rare spatterings of ink. The sheet of letter paper—as later the schoolboy's notebook and the drawing paper—becomes for Artaud a surface that is as much active as acted upon, a field of action combining the lettering—fully thought out, it seems—of the various graphic elements of the handwritten text (capital letters, Roman numerals, block letters), the layout (the placement of drawn elements at the center and at the corners of the paper, an effect of symmetry, a triangular arrangement), and finally the attack of the maculations: the burned perforations, imposed on the paper itself, the "subjectile," in order to denounce its inertia and impotence. Altogether the ensemble already has the appearance of a votive "image" of an infernal realm. At the same time it possesses the function of exorcism, the theatricality of which is evident: the double sign of the Cross superimposed on the spell sent to Jacqueline Lamba constitutes a sacred gesture of protection (recalling that of the monk—played by Artaud—brandishing a crucifix over Joan of Arc's head in Carl Dreyer's film); the traces of burns are obvious acts of aggression and purification.

Effective in a different way are the spells sent out in 1939 from the Ville-Évrard asylum: their imprecatory violence now resides more in the physical state of the missive than in the words. Inscribed with a thick ink crayon in purple, the different signs (crosses, stars, triangles, spirals in the shape of serpents, the cabalistic significance of which Artaud well knew) proliferate in all directions, invade the center of the paper itself, break the continuous thread of writing drawn with the same ink crayon: fragments of writing and drawn pictograms henceforth form one body. Not only that: knots, amorphous clusters of crayon, seem to respond in counterpoint, proceeding from the same charge of aggression, to the holes produced by burning the paper (the edges of which are also ravaged); and traces of violent shades of yellow, blue, and red (Artaud also knew the symbolism of colors: these are the colors of death) intensify by their physical presence the imprecatory force of the words. These are no

1
A word of African origin meaning a charm, fetish, or amulet.—ed.

2
Cahiers d'Art, no. 5 (1927).

longer simple votive letters but true magical objects, to be handled while making ritualistic gestures (the spell to Léon Fouks [cat. no. 4]), which can "illuminate themselves," like "gris-gris."[1]

Tattoos of colored signs inscribed on the paper, perforations made by burning the body of the paper itself: the "melding" of these two processes—painting and fire—long since adopted by Artaud, takes on the nature of revelation for him. Speaking in 1925 of André Masson's painting, he said he saw "cocoons of fire" lacerating human entrails, which were to be deciphered like those of a sacrifice. In "L'Automate personnel," he admires the painting of Jean de Bosschère, which he considers "a world cut open, a naked world, full of filaments and strips, where the inflaming force of fire lacerates the interior firmament, the tearing apart of the mind."[2] Once again, he highlights the role of fire in the fascination that Lucas van Leyden's painting *Lot and His Daughters* (c. 1509) exerts on him; its analysis initiates his reflection on the exorcising, operative function—destructive, constructive—of "true" theater, that in which or by which an original tongue is rediscovered. The language of fire or the fire of language: all the same for the founder of the Theater of Cruelty, the "fires" of the footlights forming a symbolic dividing line, beyond which no compromise can take place.

For Artaud, returned from Mexico where Indians of the scorched land of the Tarahumara had taught him the purifying function of fire (a sorcerer was burned there for having believed in several gods), and in despair over an "impossible" work, fire comes to be invested with the ultimate power, that of symbolically effecting the total Destruction of the Universe, "but consciously and in revolt"; in certain spells, the central place of the number 9, the cabalistic number of infernal destruction, is significant. In 1937, in *The New Revelations of Being,* where his own name, his individual identity, his writer's signature disappear, Artaud declares: "burning is a magic act and . . . one must consent to burning, burning in advance and immediately, not one thing, but *all that for us represents things,* so as not to expose oneself to burning completely. All that is not burned by all of Us and that does not make Us *Desperates* and *Loners*, the Earth will burn."[3] Beyond the urge for self-destruction, these "cruel" letters that are the spells manifest a necessity to conjur, to exorcise a curse. They fully set in motion the blaze of writing that is finally freed—"this atmospheric thunder, this lightning"—at Rodez after 1945, the ash and blood conflagration of pictogram remnants and charred faces that will appear on the large sheets of drawing paper.

"It was in 1939, at the Ville-Évrard asylum, that I constructed my first gris-gris; on little sheets of gridded paper torn from a schoolboy's notebook I composed passive figures, like heads ravaged by fits of asthma, torments, and hiccups."[4] Confined at Ville-Évrard and then, beginning in 1943, at Rodez, doomed to silence and oblivion, Artaud drew "figures" instead of writing, constructed new spells on sheets of paper, but this time for his personal use; his "gris-gris" have for him a curative, protective, offensive function against the "demons" assailing him: "what one sees here are totems, the weapons I take up the moment I awake." Of this production only a few drawings executed in early 1944 remain. The cabalistic signs (notably ∞, the infinity sign, but also the sign of apocalyptic

O.C. 7, 145–74. [3]

O.C. 14, 148. [4]

Destruction) now occupy by themselves the surface of the sheet: a type of drawn "hieroglyphs," made up of crosses or other geometric lines, and arranged in a repetitive symmetry—a permanent echo of the signs Artaud saw in the land of the Tarahumara—from now on constitute the basic ideograms of a primary language, first steps toward the physical sign language that he attempted to create in the theater. Here signs emerge from his breath, syncopated by "asthmas" and "hiccups." Inscribed at the center of this sort of geometric architecture are skulls, as though imprisoned. Was this a reference to the human skulls lodged in the stone niches of Roquepertuse at the gates of Marseille, with which, being so well known, Artaud must have been familiar? A multiplicity of other references could be found in the immured figures of sacred pre-Columbian sanctuaries. For, faced as he is at Rodez with the tragic loss of himself, a "man suicided by society" through institutional confinement, Artaud seeks to rediscover the primary forces of ancestral creation, attempting to update the forms and meaning of an archaic visual language that traces its roots to the depths of time.

Translated by Jeanine Herman

"Les figures sur la page inerte…"

ANTONIN ARTAUD : FEBRUARY 1947

The figures on the inert page said nothing beneath my hand. They offered themselves to me like millstones that would not inspire drawing, and that I could plumb, carve, scrape, file, seam together and sunder, hack, slash to ribbons, and score without the surface ever thereby crying uncle.

Which is to say, knowing no more about drawing than about nature, I had made up my mind to coax out those forms, lines, outlines, shadows, colors, features that, as in modern painting, would represent nothing and would moreover not claim to be integrated in accordance with whatsoever visual or material law, but would create, as it were, above the paper a kind of counter-figure that would be an ongoing protest against the laws of the created object.

The goal of all these drawn and colored figures was to exorcize the curse, to vituperate bodily against the exigencies of spatial form, of perspective, of measure, of equilibrium, of dimension and, via this vituperative act of protest, to condemn the psychic world which, like a crab louse, digs its way into the physical, and, like an incubus or succubus, claims to have given it shape. . . .

And the figures that I thereby made were spells—which, after so meticulously having drawn them, I put a match to.

Translated by Richard Sieburth

Les figures sur la page inerte ne disaient rien sous ma main. Elles s'offraient à moi comme des meules qui n'inspireraient pas le dessin, et que je pouvais sonder, tailler, gratter, limer, coudre, découdre, écharper, déchiqueter et couturer sans que jamais par père ou par mère le subjectile se plaignît.

Je veux dire qu'ignorant aussi bien le dessin que la nature je m'étais résolu à sortir des formes, des lignes, des traits, des ombres, des couleurs, des aspects qui, ainsi qu'on le fait dans la peinture moderne, ne représentassent rien, et ne réclamassent pas non plus d'être réunis suivant les exigences d'une loi visuelle, ou matérielle quelconque, mais créassent comme au-dessus du papier une espèce de contre-figure qui serait une protestation perpétuelle contre la loi de l'objet créé.

Le but de toutes ces figures dessinées et coloriées était un exorcisme de malédiction, une vitupération corporelle contre les obligations de la forme spatiale, de la perspective, de la mesure, de l'équilibre, de la dimension, et à travers cette vitupération revendicatrice une condamnation du monde psychique incrusté comme un morpion sur le physique qu'il incube ou succube en prétendant l'avoir formé. . . .

Et les figures donc que je faisais étaient des sorts—que je brûlais avec une allumette après les avoir aussi méticuleusement dessinées.

2
Spell for Lise Deharme
5 September 1937
India ink on burned and
soiled paper
10½ x 8¼" (27 x 21 cm)
Fonds André Breton,
Bibliothèque Littéraire
Jacques Doucet, Paris

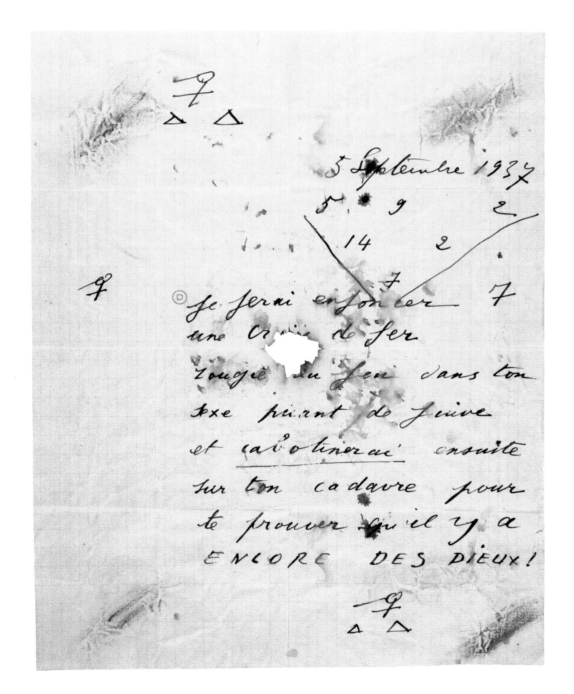

17-9-?

J'envoie un Sort
au Premier qui osera
vous toucher.
Je lui mettrai, en bouillie
sa petite gueule de faux coq
orgueilleux.
Je le fesserai devant
100 000 personnes!
SA PEINTURE QUI N'A
JAMAIS RIEN EU DE TRÈS
ÉCLATANT EST DEVENUE
DEFINITIVEMENT
MAUVAISE
IL A UNE TROP LAIDE
VOIX
C'EST L'ANTECHRIST

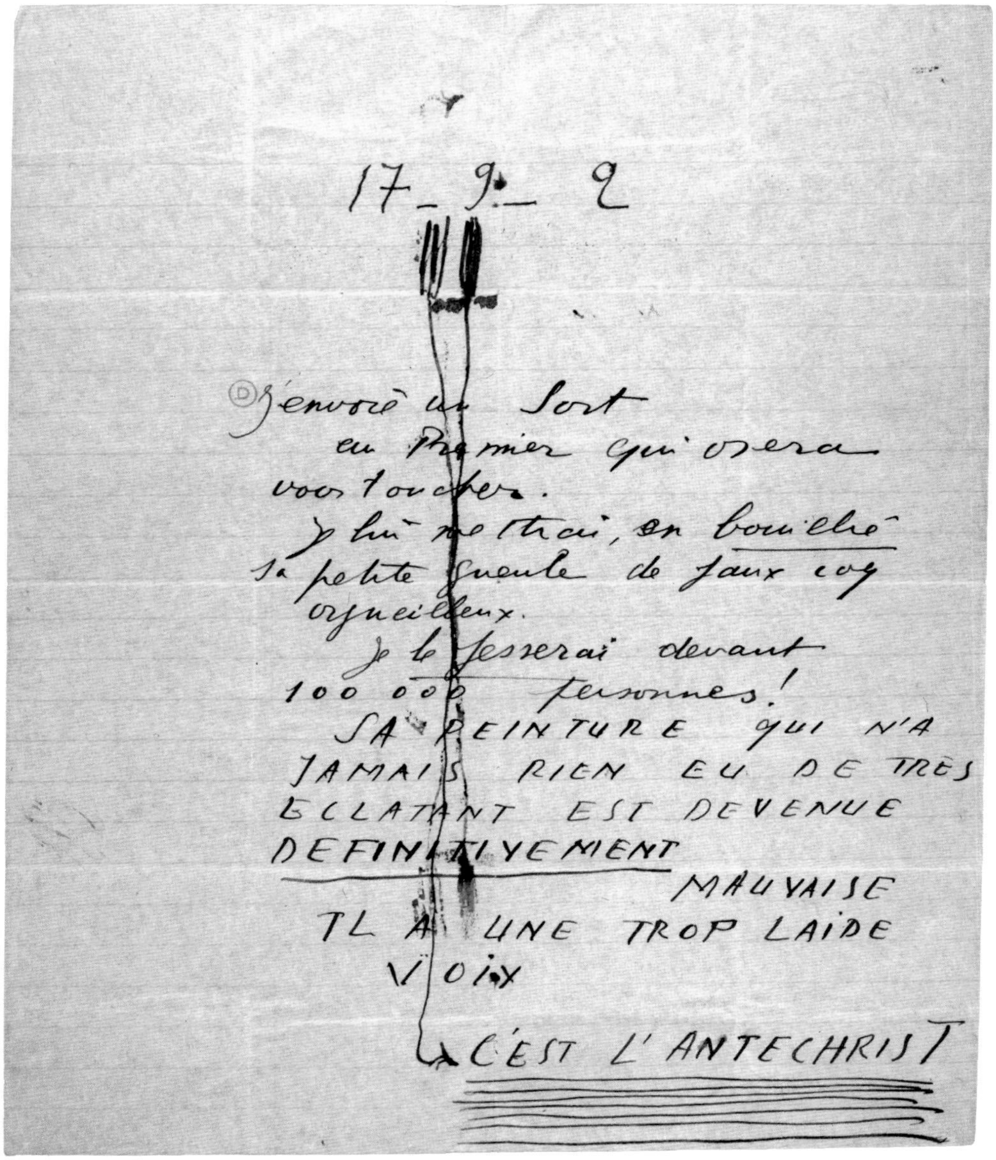

3
Spell for
Jacqueline Breton
17 September 1937
India ink
9¾ x 7⅞" (25 x 20 cm)
Fonds André Breton,
Bibliothèque Littéraire
Jacques Doucet, Paris

4
Spell for Léon Fouks
8 May 1939
Wax crayon on
burned paper
8¼ x 5¼" (21 x 13.5 cm)
Private collection

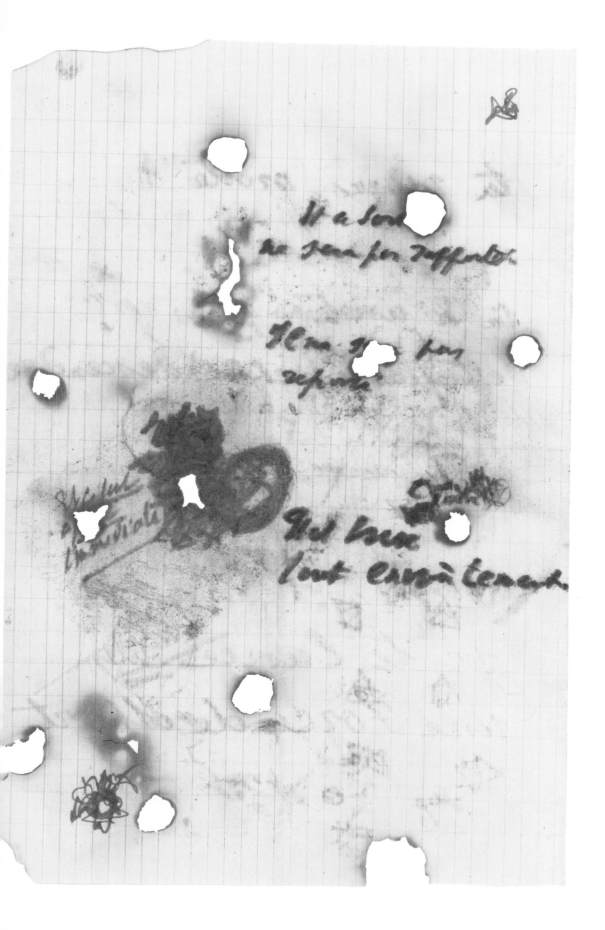

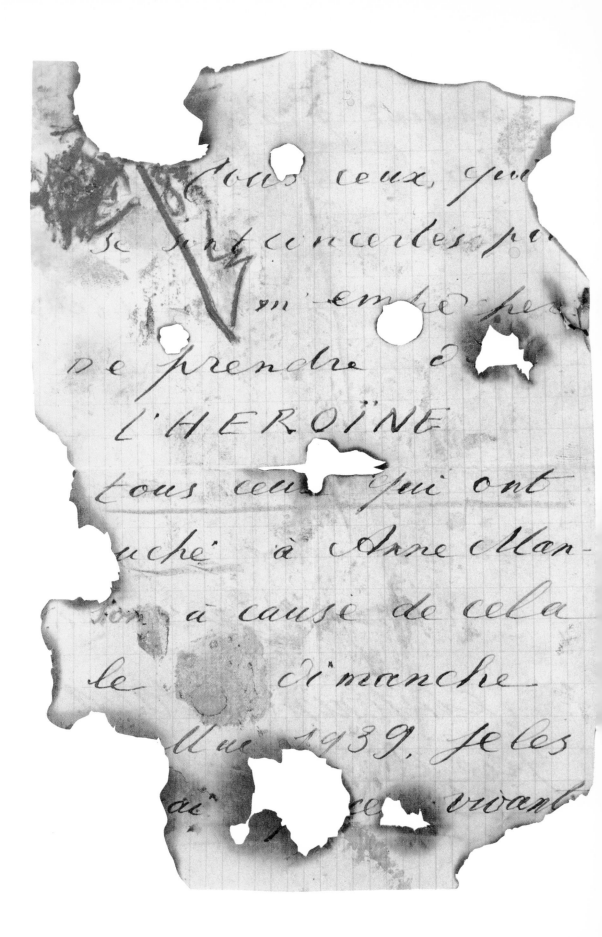

6 (recto-verso)
Spell for Roger Blin
c. 22 May 1939
Ink, wax crayon, and
gouache on burned paper
8¼ x 5¼" (21 x 13.5 cm)
Bibliothèque Nationale
de France. Bequest of
Paule Thévenin, 1994

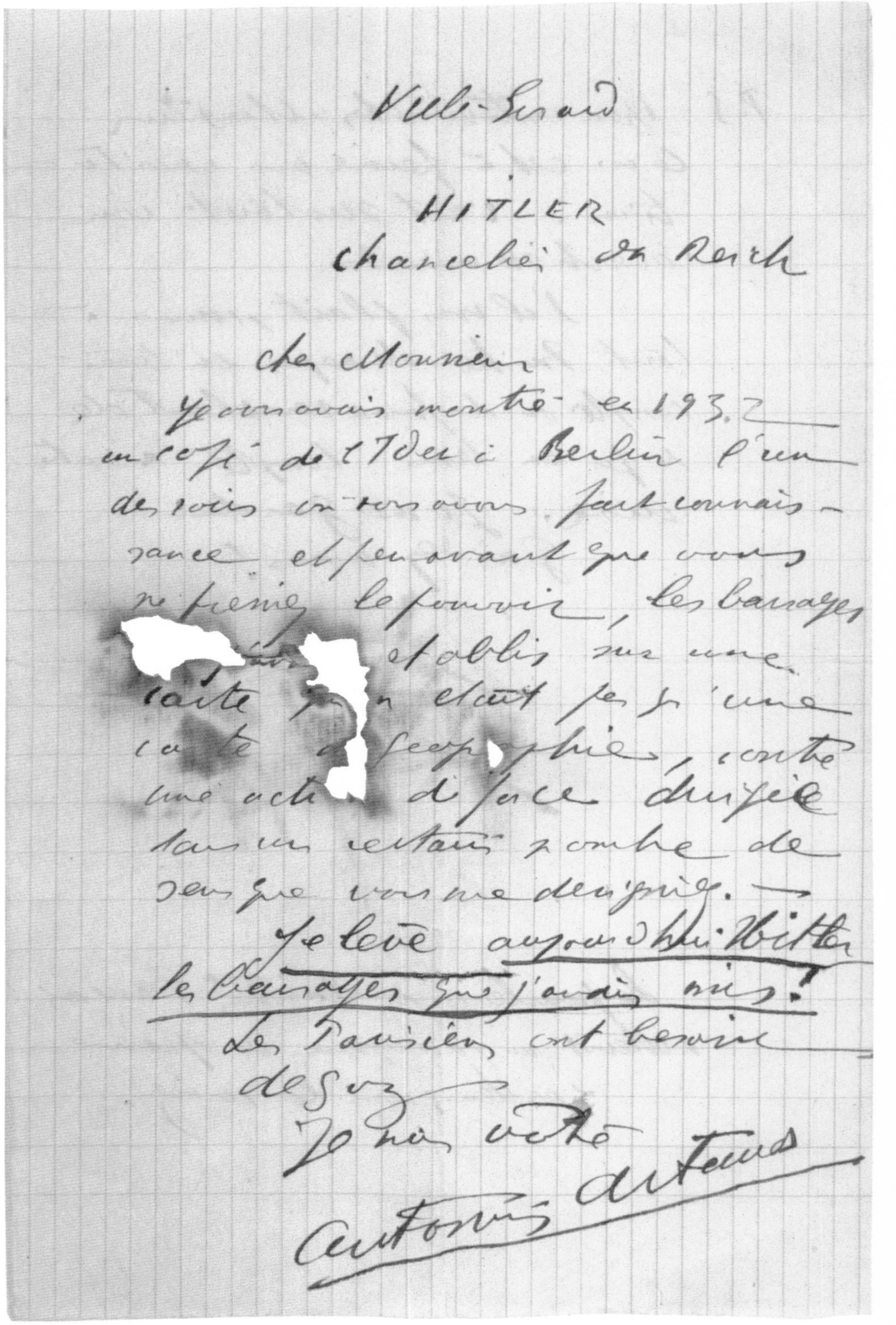

7 (recto-verso)
Spell for Hitler
c. September 1939
Wax crayon on burned paper
8¼ x 5¼" (21 x 13.5 cm)
Private collection

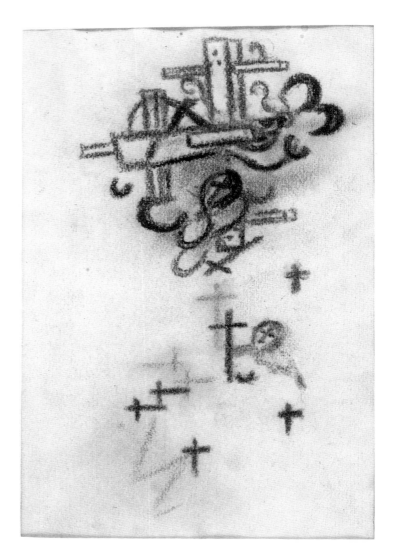

8
Untitled
c. February 1944
Charcoal
10½ x 7⅛" (27 x 18 cm)
Private collection

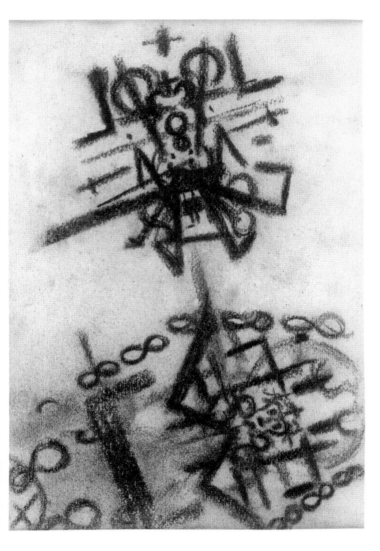

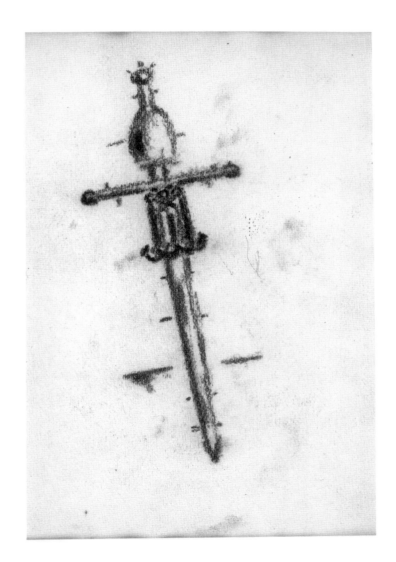

9
Untitled
c. February 1944
Charcoal
10¼ x 6⅝" (26.5 x 17.5 cm)
Musée National d'Art Moderne—
Centre de Création Industrielle,
Centre Georges Pompidou, Paris.
Bequest of Paule Thévenin, 1993

10
Untitled
c. February 1944
Charcoal
10¼ x 6⅝" (26.5 x 17.5 cm)
Musée National d'Art Moderne—
Centre de Création Industrielle,
Centre Georges Pompidou, Paris.
Bequest of Paule Thévenin, 1993

II. The Rodez Drawings

JANUARY 1945 – MAY 1946

*The psychiatric hospital at Rodez where Artaud was a patient,
1943–46.*

Agnès de la Beaumelle

"A deportee in France" for close to eight years—years of institutional confinement and misery: Les Quatre Mares, Sainte-Anne, Ville-Évrard, Chezal-Benoît, and, starting in 1943, Rodez—Antonin Artaud undertook at the beginning of 1945 the reconstruction—on a different *level*, that of the true life of the body and the mind—of his own dispossessed and devastated being, which had become itself the locus of a theater of cruelty still in its early stages, and of whose regenerating powers he never ceased to speak. The true plague is now here—the taking away of his freedom by society, the destruction of his ego by electroshocks—and, against this, he erected new defenses, created new weapons, those produced by the *insurrectional* language that he established: "Ten years since language departed, and in its place entered this atmospheric thunder, this lightning . . . How? By an antilogical, antiphilosophical, anti-intellectual, anti*dialectical* blast of language through the pressure of my black pencil and that's all."[1] Certainly, during the first years of confinement, he did not cease to write (letters of protest, appeals) and to draw (spells, the first "gris-gris"), but, starting in 1945, a continuous flood of words and pictograms, traced and drawn, was poured without respite into his schoolboy notebooks. Maxims, songs, glossolalia, scraps of sentences, shards of texts, scattered memories, interjections, invocations, endless lists of names and food—verbal discharges repeated endlessly like incantations—constitute the fragments of a textual work capable of "weeding out" his mind, eliminating the conventional "corseted language" that imprisons him, resisting what he calls poisons, crab lice, "daimons," that live as parasites on his being. At the same time appear the forms drawn in graphite, "hard, compact, opaque, unrestrained," that pulverize here and there the thread of writ-

ing in order to immediately make an offensive impact, redoubling that of the word. Now with dazzling energy the "thunder" of a new, cruel "tongue" resounds: a poetic tongue where, Artaud tells us, breath is at work, producing sounds, words, lines, colors, gestures, a language where writing and drawing become fully oral and immediately visible, brilliant and implacable like "the lightning I caused now by the human act of breathing, which my pencil strokes on the paper sanction."[2] The work of Artaud who writes and draws is an organic work, enacted and experienced in the body and by the body—the actor's true depiction of cruelty is there—a labor of expelling, of execrating, of belching, brought about by the breath's rhythm itself commanding the body's movements and the voice's modulations. Work where glossolalic incantations and the magic rituals of sniffling and whirling—"lunatic" practices which Dr. Ferdière, unaware of their exorcistic and constructive function, will unceasingly try to cure him of—have their part: "like magic I take my thick breath, and by means of my nose, my mouth, my hands, and my two feet I project it against everything that might bother me/And how many are there in the air now, boxes, cases, totems, gris-gris, walls, surfaces, sticks, nails, rope, and hundreds of nails, breastplates, helmets, armor, masks, carders, iron collars, winches, garottes, gallows, and dials, projected by my will!"[3]

The production of this veritable panoply of defensive and offensive weapons, the dual deployment of texts and drawings forged at the very root of lived experience, will allow him to activate once again the "machine of being." "Each sign that I trace on a drawing or that I write in a text represents in my consciousness an infinite weight to lift."[4] It allows him to rebuild an anatomy: "This drawing represents my attempt

2
Idem.

1
Luna Park, no. 5 (October 1979).

3
O.C. 14, 144–45.

4
Letter to Jean Dequeker, April 1945.

at the moment to rebuild a body with the bone of the musics of the soul."[5] This new graphic practice has a purgative, purifying function; it is a "balm" whose curative secrets, lost since antiquity, Artaud evokes.

Exercises of resistance and of disintegration/reintegration, the large "written drawings" that unfurl on separate sheets and the pictograms inscribed in the notebooks of Rodez are indissolubly linked. It must be emphasized that the elaboration of the drawings appeared before the writing of the actual texts, as if the graphic *translation* of what Artaud had to express could not be accomplished unless first in the visible and mute appearance of signs and drawn figures, as if the work of the hand that draws was the necessary driving force behind that of the hand that writes, one conditioning the other and soon the second stimulating the first, one always doubling back on the other. The first large "written" drawings of the year 1945—which are thus the inaugural experiments of his new poetic language—are in fact different from those of the last months at Rodez, where the more emphatic and more liberated drawing finds itself paralleled by the more forceful writing deployed in the notebooks, ultimately part of the same process, the same pulse.

In *"L'être et ses foetus..."* [Being and its fetuses], *"L'immaculée conception..."* [The immaculate conception], and *"Jamais réel et toujours vrai..."* [Never real and always true] [cat. nos. 11, 13, and 14], executed at the end of 1944 and the beginning of 1945, and again in certain later drawings such as *Couti l'anatomie*, *The Soldier with a Gun*, *"Les illusions de l'âme"* [The illusions of the soul], *The Minotaur*, and *The Machine of Being* [cat. nos. 15, 16 (verso), 19, 20, and 21 (verso)], the writing pencil fills the page in a uniform fashion and still lightly, with only the more emphatic accents bringing out a few pictograms. The color, initially faint and muted, becomes more and more present, bursting into scattered patches of lemon yellow, crimson, green, blue, blood-ocher, jarring patches like burn marks, the stigmata of strident pains. The writing unfolds around the borders of the sheet, composing, in a way, the signifying frame

[5]
O.C. 18, 73.

[6]
Letter to Gaston Ferdière, 28 February 1946.

[7]
O.C. 14, 26.

of a strange narrative. The words of glossolalia, also necessary to the *comprehension* of the drawing, are lodged in the empty spaces, filling them with their barbarous sonorities: "The sentences I wrote on the drawing I gave you I sought out syllable by syllable, out loud while working, to see if the verbal sonorities capable of aiding the comprehension of the one looking at my drawing had been found."[6] Continuous curves, curling back on themselves, scattered dots, rectilinear lines, define the shapeless elements as well as the figures (frontal or profile) or the pictograms. The formal basis of the drawing is therefore that of a flat rendering, surrounded by inscriptions, of frontal figures—repetitive, clumsy, as though drawn by a child. It resembles—an unconscious resurgence in Artaud, not unlike the appearance of phonemes of an ancient language—the miniatures illustrating the ancient manuscripts of the *chansons de geste* such as those of the *Apocalypse de Saint-Sever* (coll. Bibliothèque Nationale), the cruelty of which Georges Bataille had pointed out in 1930. These *chansons de geste* drawn at Rodez have the same "primary" expression, as though returning to old traditions, and, though often colored by buffoonery and truculence, they unfold the narrative of an internal battle. The body fragments and shapeless remnants of a disorganized and emptied anatomy are enumerated here in an obsessional manner: "the mutilated body is this stomach of misery that is always seeking to reassemble itself."[7] Feet, hands, bones, fetuses, decapitated heads crushed in the shape of basins, monstrous breasts, erect penises, severed limbs, stubs, intestines, exist alongside torture wheels, spikes, saw blades, cannons, rifles, scythes, denounced as so many sexual proliferations. They are juxtaposed, integrated on the surface of the sheet according to principles of symmetry, of vertical or horizontal structure, that are disrupted by the anarchic intrusion of the "crooked" (the "askew"). It is an impossible and paranoid attempt at architectonic organization—an interior, skeletal architecture, fleshless and chaotic. These drawings are singular anatomical *plates*, veritable functional supports on which Artaud lays out his struggle against the organic residues of a corporal identity that must be rebuilt: "One does not reenter one's body, the body reenters you after it has entered into itself: the unfathomable sexual heart./This heart mounted between 2 cheek-straps, but it had to be shit in order to make it shit because by force of being a heart it only wanted desire and not the suffering of pain/ Take off the cheek-straps, take up the harness, abandon the harness, take control of oneself out-side of the harness, make oneself into a harness stand and one's being into a slaughter, and in that slaughter of the heart, force it to take fire."[8]

From the moment they appear in January 1945, Artaud considers his large drawings tangible proofs of his mental health, which is not "alienated," manifestations of his recovered creative power, visible signs of his regained strength. It is thus that he shows them to the doctors at the asylum: the interest of Dr. Ferdière and Dr. Dequeker among others soon leads him to hope that he will be able to earn some money from them (determined to get out of Rodez, he expresses his wish to be able finally to support himself). It is in this light that he speaks of them to his correspondents: Jean Paulhan, Henri Thomas, Dr. Dequeker, et cetera, and that he insists on showing them to his visitors: Jean Dubuffet (September 1945), Marthe Robert and Arthur Adamov (February 1946), Henri and Colette Thomas (March 1946). The encouragement he receives—in particular from Dubuffet —strengthens his belief in having produced true *works* (on several occasions, he will list them in his notebooks), which may, in the same way as the publication of his books, bring him income. His drawings are thus destined to be seen, "received" (and their commentaries heard), and not, like those of the notebooks, devoted solely to a private daily exercise. From this time in particular, with the lucidity that had always been his, he detects their profound singularity and makes a claim for their significance: "These are," he writes to Jean Paulhan on January 10, 1945, "written drawings, with sentences that are inserted into the forms in order to activate them. I think I have arrived at something special, as in my books or in the theater."

Artaud is conscious of possessing here the

seeds—the "principles," he says—of an original, powerful expression that intimately links not only writing and drawing (even when they are separate activities, they originate in the same creative act) but, as on the theatrical stage, visual, oral, and corporal effects—in order to constitute on the page a signifying, effective whole, the *total act* that he had looked for since the early 1930s from the Theater of Cruelty and whose power of *signification* ought to equal for him that of certain paintings. Linear tracings, vibrations of colors, sonorities of inscribed words—the physical manifestations of the artist's gesture—work together to produce an overall effect, which makes sense and acts directly, physically and mentally, on himself— a curative effect—and on the spectator—a revelatory effect. They are like *compositions* in the musical, pictorial, and alchemical senses of the word: "The drawings of which I am speaking to you are full of latent forms, in the stumbling itself of the pencil's line, and I wanted them to *work in concert* with each other so that with the colors, the shadows, and their emphases the whole would become valid and singular."[9] And further: "Not the colors but the *melody* that they summon from one another, not the forms but the improbable body that they seek through the infinity of an arbitrary expanse." It is of some interest to recall that, prepared to start drawing again at Dr. Ferdière's instigation, Artaud very specifically evokes the "theoretical" work of the Alfred Jarry Theater, as he had attempted to define it in 1930 using "tableaux vivants" created with the help of photomontages: "I made a lot of surrealist photographs at the time. I made some with Elie Lotar. And even in a studio with electric lights and all the necessary elements, it takes hours of preparation to manage to extract an *eloquent poetic figure*, especially from an assemblage of inanimate objects."[10] In these "tableaux vivants," sectioned human limbs and decapitated bodies were seen strewn about a the-atrical space—the "black hole" of a fireplace represented the framework of a stage—and already constituted the vivid, incandescent logs and embers for what would become the future Theater of Cruelty. These logs and embers, fixed

8
O.C. 20, 19.

9
Letter to Henri Thomas, 12 February 1946.

10
Letter to Gaston Ferdière, 18 October 1943.

here and there on the scenic expanse of the Rodez drawings' sheets, correspond to the scattered limbs, animated by the secret music of an infernal dance: evocative poetic figures, born of an exercise experienced this time within the body. "I want it to be the body that makes the furnace and not the furnace that makes the body and the body is not a long patience but a dreadful impatience always ignited, and not dead bodies fallen from patience with time."[11]

Still more acted and active are the drawings executed at the end of 1945 and the beginning of 1946: *"Poupou rabou...," "La bouillabaisse de formes dans la tour de babel"* [The bouillabaisse of forms in the tower of Babel], *"La maladresse sexuelle de dieu"* [The sexual awkwardness of god], *"Le théâtre de la cruauté"* [The theater of cruelty], *The Inca*, and *"L'exécration du Père-Mère"* [The execration of the Father-Mother] [cat. nos. 17, 23–26, and 29]. The same residual anatomical fragments are there, but amplified, dramatized, captured as though under a magnifying glass in their secret gestation; occupying in close-up the center of the sheet, they become powerful signs: "the theater of cruelty wants to make eyelids dance two by two with elbows, kneecaps, thigh bones, toes, and for one to see it."[12] Whereas the glossolalic phonemes have practically disappeared, the black and oily weight of the graphite henceforth inscribes their wounding, sonorous matter onto the sheet, the colors striate the space, make it vibrate, fill the forms with new life or unfold as hieroglyphic signs identical to those of that "land of painting" that the Sierra Tarahumara represented for Artaud. The lines ultimately create scarifications on the body of the paper itself, the forms become menacing instruments: chests, canines, iron collars, coffins enclosing human skeletons, while, thus embedded, encircled, human heads emerge. The sheet of the drawing as a whole becomes a *sensitive plate* with variable intensities, on which unstable and disoriented elements are scattered—"between the two positive and negative poles of the bones of the Father-Mother the heart explodes"[13]: it is, indeed, as Artaud insists, "to be looked at sideways." The earlier schizophrenic obsession with order and repetition no

longer exists: an effect of inner chaos, the graphic chaos is there, brutally hurled and at the same time skillfully orchestrated by a hand that incises and blurs everything in turn—the hand of a man of the theater—and shaped by a voice that is strident but controls its modulations. This chaos laid bare and flayed open, yet suppressed, possesses the power to reveal truths unfathomed until now. Like the vitriolic, burnt pages of the years 1937–39, which Artaud called his spells and gris-gris, the drawings have a real exorcistic function and must emit magic powers: such as the drawing (lost today, whose execution Artaud mentions in a notebook of Febuary 1946) titled *The Pentacle* (an ancient talisman in the shape of a five-pointed star, bearing cabalistic signs), which could be either of two drawings, *"Le théâtre de la cruauté" or "L'exécration du Père-Mère,"* where the epidermis of the paper, slashed by lines, becomes the transposed medium of this central wound that is the birth of the body, a transfer, finally enacted and execrated, of the original suffering. "This drawing," Artaud says, "is intentionally spoiled, thrown on the page in contempt of forms and lines, in order to show contempt for the original idea and to succeed in neutralizing it."[14]

After these graphic works, so completely physical, skillful and clumsy, which come to resonate closely with the bursts of poetic writing scattered on the pages of the notebooks, one might be surprised by the almost "cerebral" aspect and graphic poverty of some of the drawings that follow: *Man and His Pain* and *Death and Man*, executed in April 1946 [cat nos. 27 and 28]. The dryness of the line and the colors almost confers upon them the appearance and function of abstract symbols. Drawing becomes only a *translation*, a visual metaphor, that addresses itself no longer solely to the eye or to the ear but, as Artaud insists, to the *mind* directly, a reconstruction of the *consciousness* of "a sensation that passed through him and that he wanted to transmit as stripped bare": a sensation captured in its germination and latent state, which finds its expression in a line that is lean and lifeless, like his mechanical, puppetlike body. It is significant that Artaud would have felt the need to intensify

11
O.C. 16, 176.

14
O.C. 20, 173.

12
O.C. 13, 288.

13
O.C. 16, 176.

and strengthen the cerebral resonance of these drawings with several written commentaries, at the same time regarding them as tentative and awkward explanations. For it was important for him to stay as close as possible to the lived and the perceived, to remain close to their "metaphysics," to restore "the idea" rooted in the tangible: "I wanted the torment and exhaustion of the seeker's consciousness in the midst of and around his idea to take on meaning for once, to be received and be part of the completed work, for in this work there is an idea."[15] Not only the "pathetic awkwardness" claimed in the first drawings at Rodez—the "bouillabaisse" of forms, the stumbling of the pencil, the spoiling of the "subjectile" (the stained, incised, crumpled paper of *The Machine of Being*), but now the poverty and diminishment (fully accepted and *concerted* as well) of the graphic expression—this "loss" that is at the center of all his creation, that makes his drawings what they are, Artaud insists, "miseries," *transfer drawings*—become the essential modes of this primary "language" finally achieved at Rodez, a drawn and written, breathing and pulsing language that enters into resonance with the body, nourishes and replenishes it. It is poetic language—at once concrete and abstract, intuitive and learned, expressive and cerebral—captured at the source of the "tetème," a symbolic breast-feeding effected in the innermost depths and necessary to the rebirth of the "inborn totem" of man.

The active sonorities of these "primary" words used by Artaud must be heard, made to reverberate with the emphatic pictograms of certain drawings like *Couti l'anatomie*, or with the dry signs displayed in *Man and His Pain* or *Death and Man*, in order to understand the functioning of this totally new endeavor of regenerating the original gestation of body and mind:

And what is the tetème? *the blood of the body stretched out at that moment and which is dozing for it is sleeping. How is the* tetème *blood. Through the sema, before which the T is resting and designates that which is resting like the* té vé *of those who live in Marseille. For the* té *makes a noise of ashes when the tongue deposits it in the*

[15]
O.C. 19, 259.

[16]
"Fragments,"
L'Arche, no. 16
(June 1946).

lips where it will smoke. And Ema *in Greek means blood. And* tetème *two times ash over the flame of the clot of blood, this inveterate clot of blood that is the body of the sleeper who is dreaming and would do better to awaken. For neither the unconscious nor the subconscious are the law. Each dream is a piece of pain wrested from us, by other beings, at random by the hand of a monkey that they throw on me every night, the resting ash of our self which is not ash but hammers like the blood is scrap iron and the self is ferruginous. And what is the ferruginous? It is this simple: a head a trunk on two legs and two arms to shake the trunk in the direction of ever more being with a head, two legs and two arms. For it has always been said that the illiterate is a mystery without alpha and without omega, but with a head, two legs, two arms. The hopeless illiterate simpleton that is man and does not understand. He understands that he is head and arms, legs in order to set the trunk in motion. And that there is nothing outside of this: the totem of the ears eyelids and a nose drilled by twenty fingers. And this is the mystery of man that god the spirit does not stop pestering. And this body is a fact: me—there is no inside, no spirit, no outside or consciousness, nothing but the body such as we see it a body that does not cease to be even when the eye that sees it falls. And this body is a fact: me.*[16]

Artaud, the *mômo*, who before his departure in May 1946 from Rodez was able to reconstruct a human head on drawing paper (*The Blue Head*) [cat. no. 33] and identify himself finally in a first *Self-Portrait* [cat. no. 32]—a field of death brought to life, a lunar Pierrot—is indeed this illiterate who is no longer seeking a style, "has abandoned the principle of drawing." Faced with the "monkey hand" placed on him—the terror of history, the terror of society and of the organic body—he erects his insurrectional "simpleton's" language, which is "a verb, a grammar, an arithmetic, an entire Cabala that shits at the other, that shits on the other." These exercises of cruelty and meditation that are the Rodez writings and drawings, splendid and arid corporal and spiritual exercises, allow the cast shadows, the incandescent remnants of the territories of gestation of a lost "human" world to be seen and heard—and understood—in a dazzling poetic clarity that will not leave him until his death. What Artaud discovers, this anarchist finally liberated, and what upon leaving Rodez he permits us to see on the veritable genetic maps of waves of varying intensities and densities that are his drawings, is a new *perception* of the "innate" being: the consciousness of the body and of the mind not as an individual or social organism, constituted and signifying, but as a stripped, live *field*, open, crossed by circuits, passages, fluxes, connections, resonances, forces of death and life, and, finally, of multiple becomings.

Translated by Jeanine Herman

"Mes dessins ne sont pas des dessins…"

ANTONIN ARTAUD : RODEZ, APRIL 1946

My drawings are not drawings but documents.
You must look at them and understand what's *inside*.
Judge them only from the standpoint of art or
truthfulness as you would a telling and consummate
object and you'll say:
This is all very well, but there is a lack of
manual and technical training and as a draftsman
Mr. Artaud is only a beginner, he needs ten years of
personal apprenticeship or at the polytechnic of fine arts.
Which is false, for I have worked at drawing
for *ten* years in the course of my entire existence,
but I *despair* of pure drawing.
I mean that there is in my drawings a sort of music
moral that I have made by living my strokes, not with the
hand only but with the rasping of the breath of my
trachea and the teeth of my mastication.
—And these are not things to be seen through
a microscope, but neither are they things
to be seen if one insists on seeing them under the lid of
this *nature* angle.
I mean to say that we are filmy-eyed because our
current ocular vision is *deformed*, repressed, oppressed,
reverted and suffocated by certain malversations
on the principle of our brain-case, as on the dental
architecture of our being, from the coccyx at the bottom of the
vertebral column, to the foundations of the forceps of the
maxillaries sustaining the brain.
Struggling against these malversations I have
stippled and chiselled all the angers of my struggle

Mes dessins ne sont pas des dessins mais des documents,
il faut les regarder et comprendre ce qu'il y a *dedans*,
à ne les juger que du point de vue artistique ou
véridique, objet parlant et réussi,
on dirait:
cela est très bien mais ça manque de formation manuelle et
technique et M. Artaud comme dessinateur n'est encore qu'un
débutant, il lui faut dix ans d'apprentissage personnel ou à la
poly-technique des beaux-arts.
Ce qui est faux car j'ai travaillé *dix* ans le dessin au
cours de toute mon existence mais je me suis *désespéré*
du pur dessin.
Je veux dire qu'il y a dans mes dessins une espèce de
morale musique que j'ai faite en vivant mes traits non avec
la main seulement, mais avec le raclement du souffle de ma
trachée-artère, et des dents de ma mastication.
—Et ce ne sont pas des choses qui se voient au
microscope, mais ce ne sont pas non plus des choses qui se
voient si on veut s'obstiner à les voir sous la chape de cet
angle *nature*.
Je veux dire que nous avons une taie sur l'oeil du
fait que notre vision oculaire actuelle est *déformée*, réprimée,
opprimée, revertie et suffoquée par certaines malversations
sur le principe de notre boîte cranienne, comme sur
l'architecture dentaire de notre être, depuis le coccyx du bas
des vertèbres, jusqu'aux assises du forceps des mâchoires
sustentatrices du cerveau.
Luttant contre ces malversations j'ai pointillé et
buriné toutes les colères de ma lutte en vue d'un certain

in view of a number of totems of being and
these miseries, my drawings, are all that is left.
But there is more, namely
that this struggle in its *essence* doesn't cease
being concretely signified by lines and
points.
These points are strewn on the page.
These lines are what you could call
interstitial lines.
Interstitial they are, as though
suspended within the
movement they accompany,
movement that jostles against the breath,
like shadows at the bottom of a hollow, which would
not only be its shadow
but one more living being
and which play then from shadow to shadow
above the hollow's head.
An emotion is added thus,
something like the framework of the hair of
an emotion naturally produced
(as one says: there's a hair in there), of
the emotion generating the drawings, I mean,
and that whoever looks at my drawings must
superadd this primal emotion subordinated by
nature on pain of becoming no more than an
incompetent illiterate.

Translated by Roger McKeon

nombre de totems d'êtres, et il en reste
ces misères, mes dessins.
Mais il y a quelque chose de plus:
c'est que cette lutte dans son *essence* ne cesse pas
d'être signifiée concrètement par des lignes et par des
points.
Ces points sont semés sur la page.
Ces lignes sont ce qu'on pourrait appeler des
lignes *interstitielles.*
Interstitielles elles le sont, étant comme en
suspens dans le
mouvement qu'elles accompagnent,
mouvement qui bouscule le souffle,
comme des ombres au fond d'un creux qui ne
seraient pas
seulement son ombre
mais un être vivant de plus et qui jouent alors d'ombre en
ombre par-dessus la tête du creux.
Cela constitue donc une émotion de plus,
quelque chose comme le cadre du cheveu de
l'émotion naturellement produite (comme on dit:
il y a là dedans un cheveu), je veux dire
de l'émotion génératrice du dessin et que celui qui
regarde doit surajouter cette émotion première
que la nature rendit
seconde sous peine de n'être plus lui-même qu'un
analphabète incompétent.

11
"L'être et ses foetus..."
[Being and its fetuses]
c. January 1945
Graphite and wax crayon
25¼ x 19⅝" (64 x 50 cm)
Private collection

12
The Hanged Woman
(*La Pendue*)
c. January 1945
Graphite and wax crayon
25½ x 19⅝" (65 x 50 cm)
Private collection

13
"L'immaculée conception…"
[The immaculate conception]
c. January 1945
Graphite and wax crayon
24 x 18¾" (61 x 48 cm)
Private collection

15
Couti l'anatomie
c. September 1945
Graphite and wax crayon
25⅞ x 19⅝" (65.5 x 50 cm)
Musée National d'Art Moderne—
Centre de Création Industrielle,
Centre Georges Pompidou, Paris

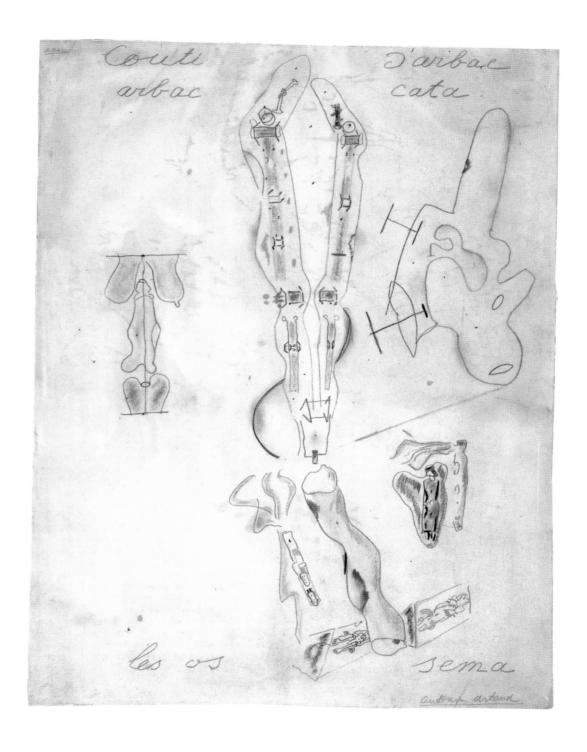

14
'Jamais réel et toujours vrai…"
[Never real and always true]
c. January 1945
Graphite and wax crayon
25¼ x 18⅞" (64 x 48 cm)
Private collection

16 (recto)
"La potence du gouffre . . ."
[The gallows for the abyss]
c. October 1945
Graphite and wax crayon
24⅞ x 18⅞" (63 x 48 cm)
Musée National d'Art Moderne—
Centre de Création Industrielle,
Centre Georges Pompidou, Paris

16 (verso)
The Soldier with a Gun
(*Le Soldat au fusil*)
c. October 1945–January 1946
Graphite and wax crayon
24⅞ x 18⅞" (63 x 48 cm)
Musée National d'Art Moderne—
Centre de Création Industrielle,
Centre Georges Pompidou, Paris

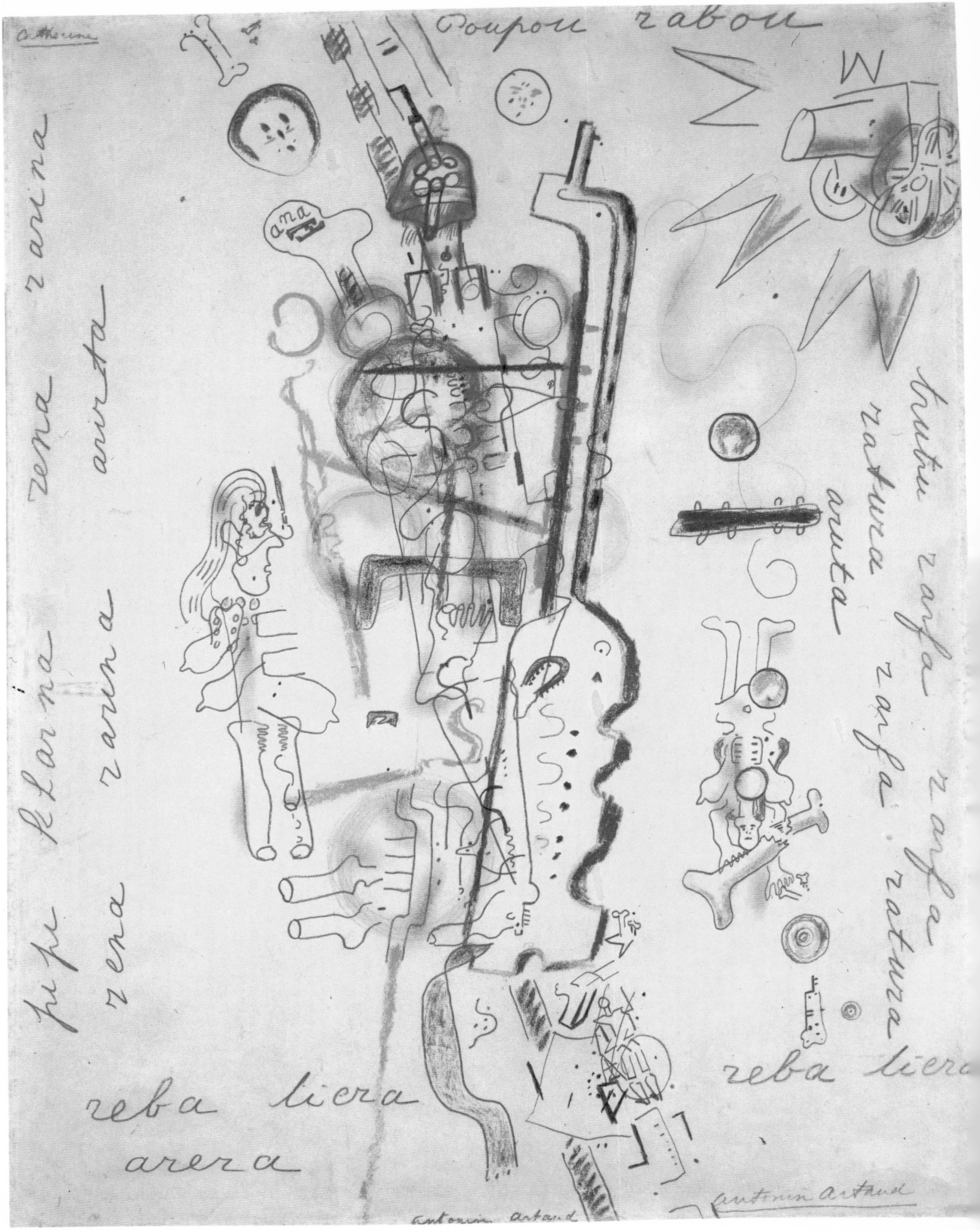

Catherine

Poupou rabou

hutu zafa zafa
ratura zafa ratura
aruta

zena zarina

aurta

hihi klarna

zena

zarina

zena

reba liera zeba liera

arera

antonin artaud   antonin artaud

18
The Totem (*Le Totem*)
c. December 1945–
February 1946
Graphite and wax crayon
24⅞ x 18⅞" (63 x 48 cm)
Musée Cantini, Marseille

17
"Poupou rabou . . ."
c. December 1945
Graphite and wax crayon
25½ x 19⅝" (65 x 50 cm)
Private collection

19
"Les illusions de l'âme"
[The illusions of the soul]
c. January 1946
Graphite and wax crayon
24⅞ x 18⅞" (63 x 48 cm)
Musée National d'Art
Moderne—Centre de
Création Industrielle,
Centre Georges Pompidou,
Paris. Gift of Michel
Ellenberger, 1987

20
The Minotaur
(*Le Minotaure*)
c. January 1946
Graphite and wax crayon
24⅞ x 18⅞" (63 x 48 cm)
Private collection

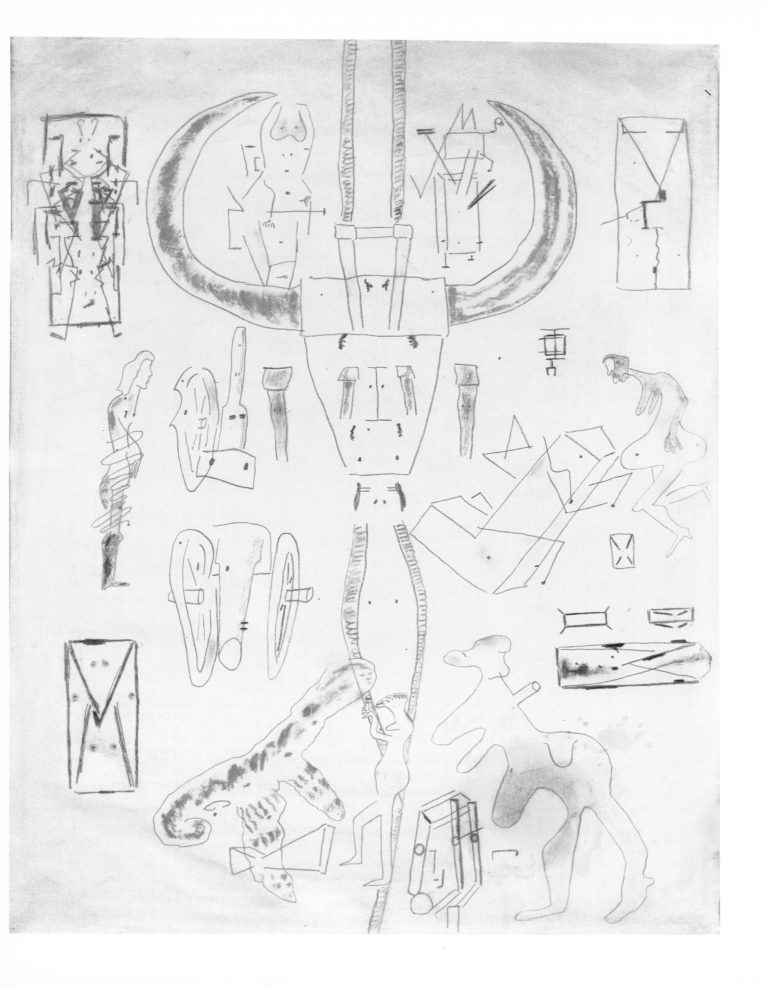

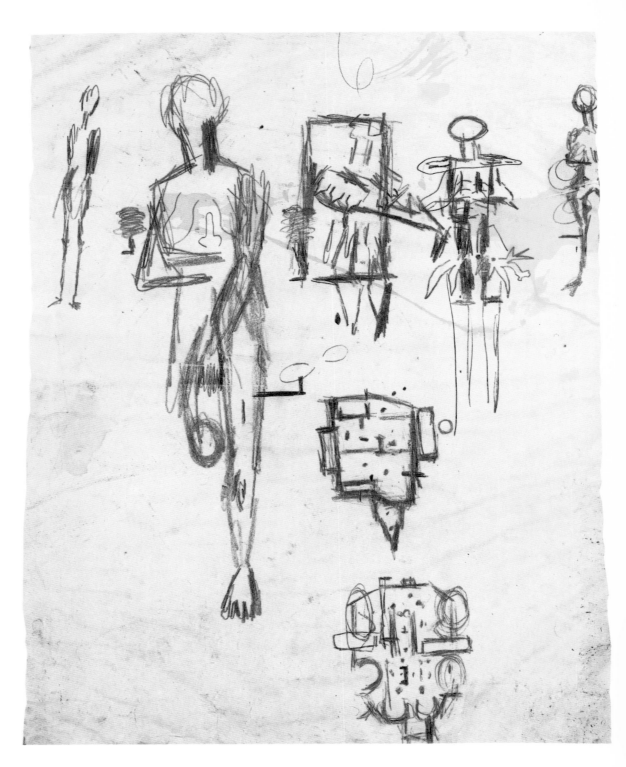

21 (recto)
Untitled
c. January 1946
Graphite
25½ x 19⅝" (65 x 50 cm)
Musée National d'Art Moderne—
Centre de Création Industrielle,
Centre Georges Pompidou, Paris

21 (verso)
The Machine of Being
(*La Machine de l'être*) or
"Dessin à regarder de traviole . . ."
[Drawing to be looked at askew]
c. January 1946
Graphite and wax crayon
25½ x 19⅝" (65 x 50 cm)
Musée National d'Art Moderne—
Centre de Création Industrielle,
Centre Georges Pompidou, Paris

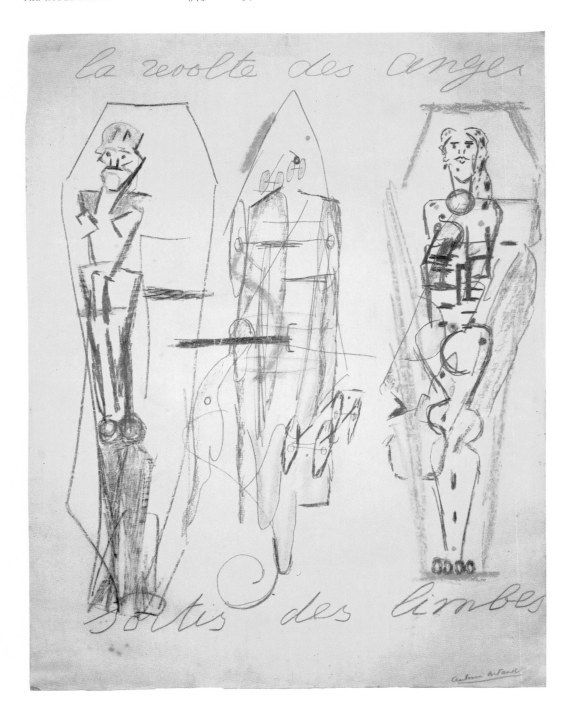

22
*"La révolte des anges sortis
des limbes"* [The revolt of the
angels exited from limbo]
c. January–February 1946
Graphite and wax crayon
25 ½ x 19 ⅝" (65 x 50 cm)
Musée Cantini, Marseille

23
"La bouillabaisse de formes
dans la tour de babel"
[The bouillabaisse of forms
in the tower of Babel]
c. February 1946
Graphite and wax crayon
24⅞ x 18⅞" (63 x 48 cm)
Private collection

24
"*La maladresse sexuelle
de dieu*" [The sexual
awkwardness of god]
c. February 1946
Graphite and wax crayon
24⅞ x 19½" (63 x 49 cm)
Private collection

25
"*Le théâtre de la cruauté*"
[The theater of cruelty]
c. March 1946
Graphite and wax crayon
24¾ x 18⅛" (62 x 46 cm)
Musée National d'Art Moderne—
Centre de Création Industrielle,
Centre Georges Pompidou, Paris.
Bequest of Paule Thévenin, 1993

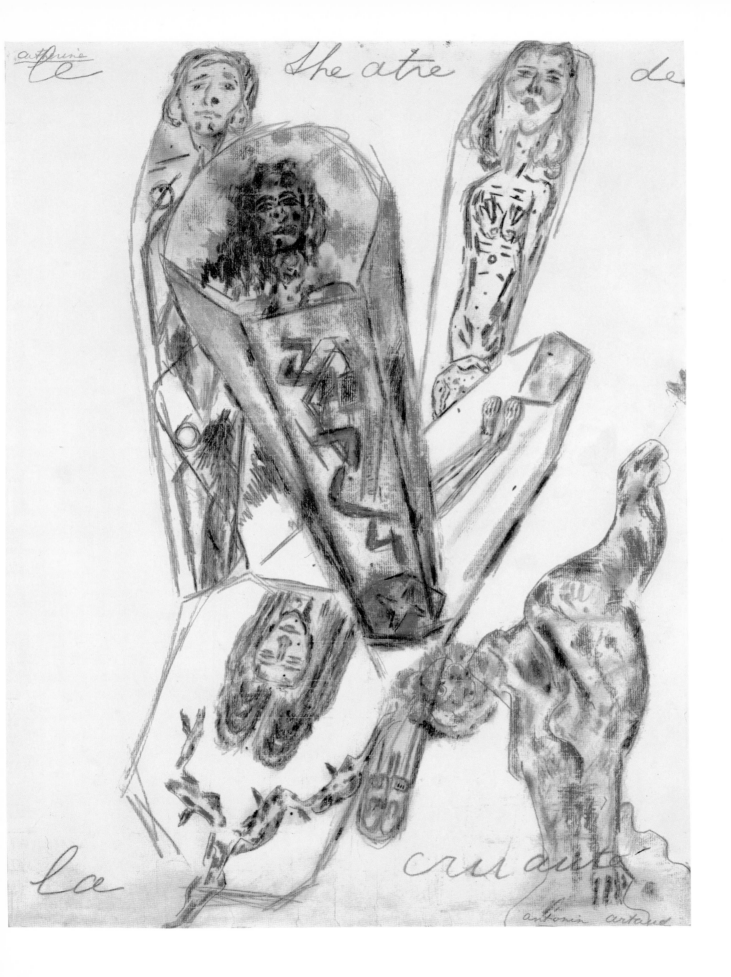

26
The Inca (L'Inca)
c. March 1946
Graphite and wax crayon
25¼ x 18⅞" (64 x 48 cm)
Musée National d'Art Moderne—
Centre de Création Industrielle,
Centre Georges Pompidou, Paris.
Bequest of Paule Thévenin, 1993

27
Man and His Pain
(*L'Homme et sa douleur*)
c. April 1946
Graphite and wax crayon
25½ x 15¼" (65 x 38.5 cm)
Musée Cantini, Marseille

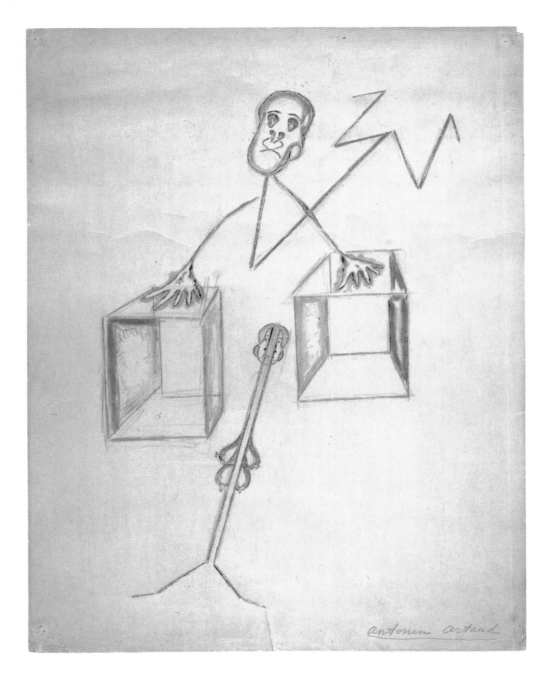

28
Death and Man
(*La Mort et l'homme*)
c. April 1946
Graphite and wax crayon
25⅞ x 20" (65.5 x 50.5 cm)
Musée National d'Art
Moderne—Centre de
Création Industrielle,
Centre Georges Pompidou,
Paris. Gift of Michel
Ellenberger, 1988

29
"L'exécration du Père-Mère"
[The execration of the
Father-Mother]
April 1946
Graphite and wax crayon
25¾ x 19¾" (64.5 x 49.5 cm)
Musée National d'Art
Moderne—Centre de
Création Industrielle, Centre
Georges Pompidou, Paris

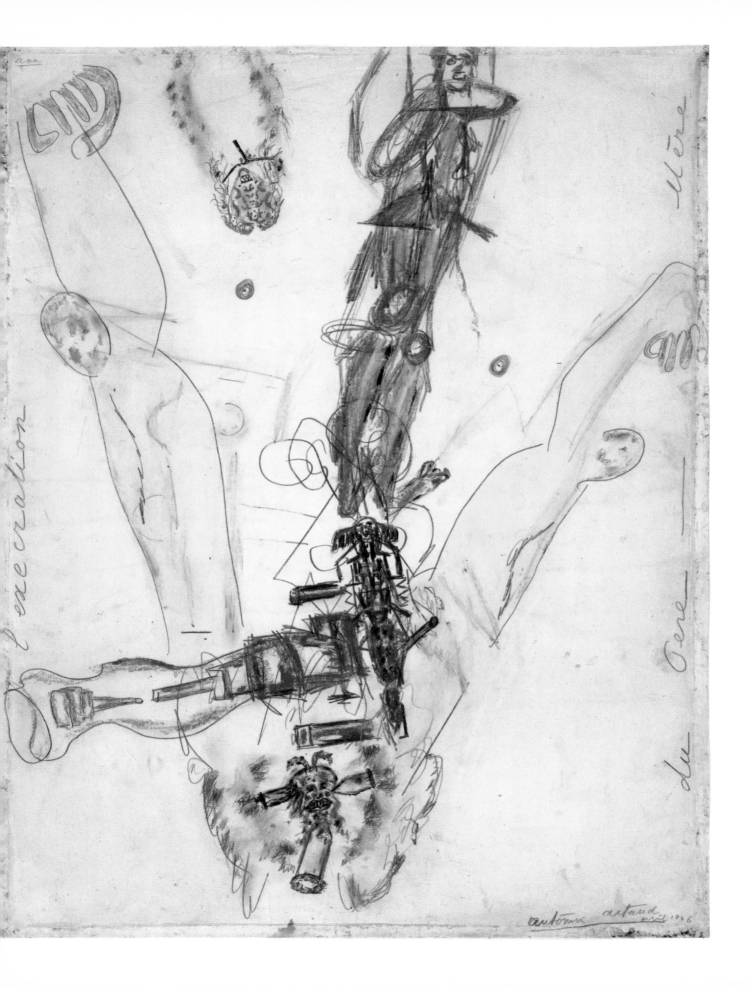

l'execration

Mère

du

Cenci

antonin artaud avril 1946

31
Earth's Bodies
(*Les Corps de terre*)
3 May 1946
Graphite and wax crayon
25¾ x 19⅞" (65.5 x 50.5 cm)
Musée National d'Art Moderne—
Centre de Création Industrielle,
Centre Georges Pompidou, Paris

30
The Whisk (*La Balayette*)
[5] May 1946
Graphite
26½ x 19⅝" (67 x 50 cm)
Private collection

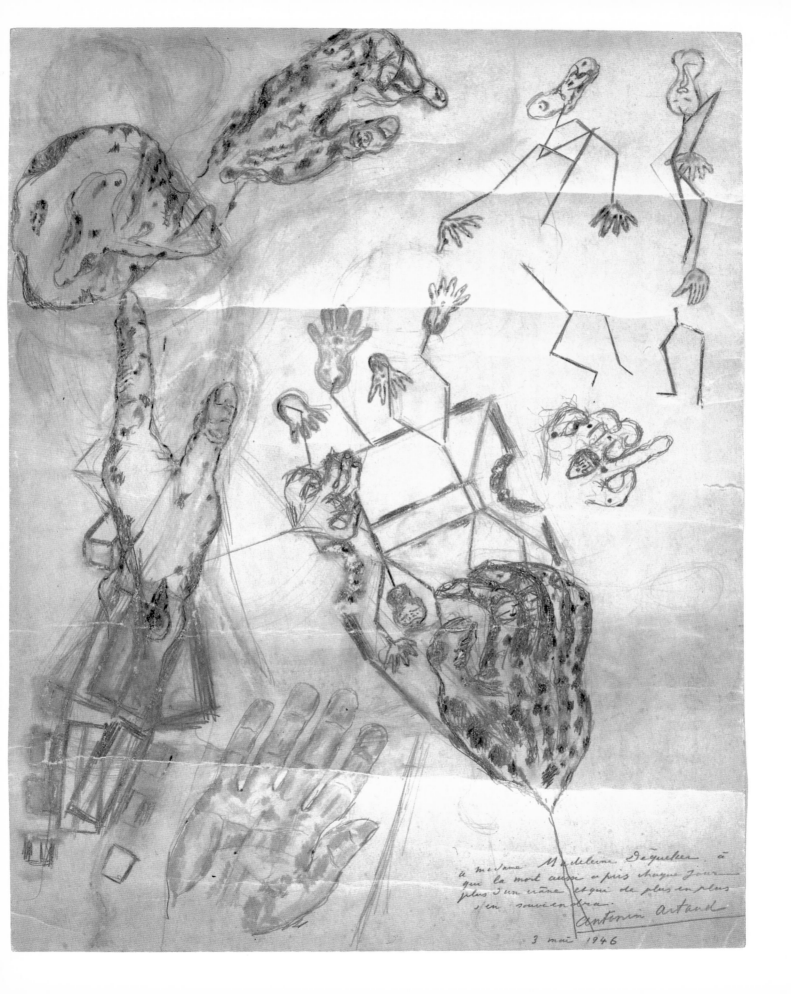

à madame Madeleine Dequeker, à
qui la mort aussi a pris chaque jour
plus d'un crâne et qui de plus en plus
s'en souviendra.
                              Antonin Artaud
        3 mai 1946

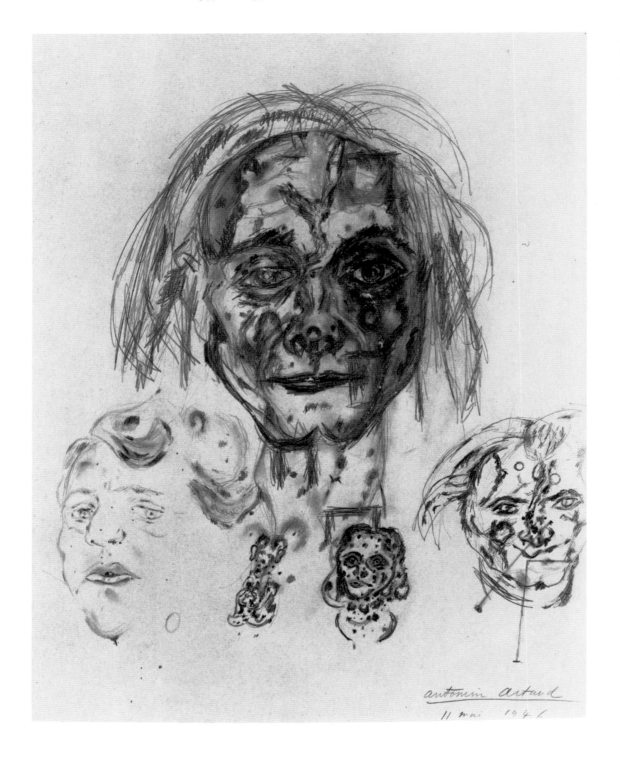

32
Self-Portrait
11 May 1946
Graphite
24⅞ x 19½" (63 x 49 cm)
Private collection

33
The Blue Head
(*La Tête bleue*)
c. May 1946
Graphite and wax crayon
24⅞ x 18⅞" (63 x 48 cm)
Musée National d'Art
Moderne—Centre de
Création Industrielle,
Centre Georges Pompidou,
Paris. Bequest of Paule
Thévenin, 1993

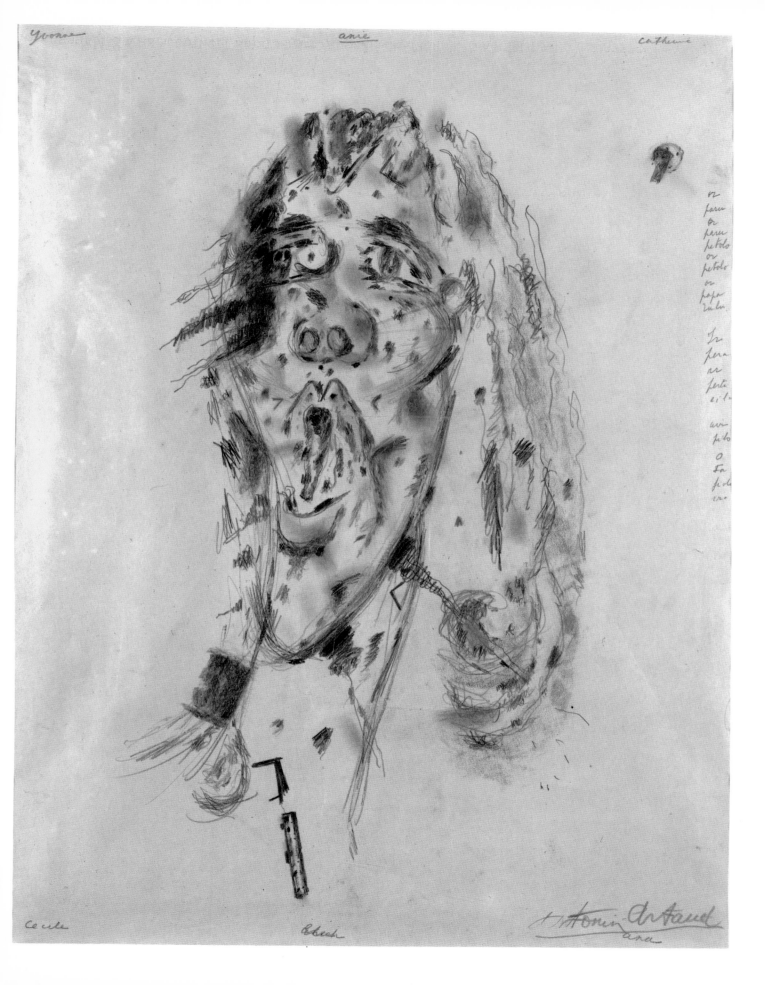

III. Portraits, Ivry

JUNE 1946 – MARCH 1948

Exterior, wing of the psychiatric clinic at
Ivry-sur-Seine where Artaud resided, 1946–48.
Photographed by Georges Pastier.

INTRODUCTION

Agnès de la Beaumelle

It begins—the hypnotic confrontation with the human face—in the last month of confinement at Rodez, May 1946, with a preliminary head, screaming and blind [*The Blue Head*, cat. no. 33] and a first *Self-Portrait* [cat. no. 32], mute and wide-eyed as it gazes into itself: faces studded with nervous knots, with sharp, vibrating lines made by the graphite pencil stippling the paper; maculated, tattooed *sur*-faces, lacerated in places, caressed in others with the shading of a finger or eraser. Stretched out and seemingly shattered by the cry that invades it, *The Blue Head* has already become a shroud, an imprint reconstructed from the shards of bodily fragmentation, which seems very likely to be that produced by electroshock, a rosy lymphatic flow, from the pain, issuing from the brain. The face in *Self-Portrait* is as implacable, its human features bearing the stigmata of the trauma that has etched it. What already stands out in these two drawings, like a necessary and lucid self-examination, possesses the force of an *ultimate* "inner experience," one through which a body, a lost bodily identity, attempts to remake itself.

The day before his release from Rodez, the author of *The Theater and Its Double* indeed seemed to have achieved, with a mastery which he would never stop trying to prove, what he had always wanted from painting: the immediate and naked *ex*-pression (in the primary sense) on paper of the disaster experienced in the depths of the self, the appearance of vestiges of a "lost world" that would have the force of truth of a "dream as hard as an insect's carapace and full of stingers darting at the sky in all directions."[1] Some forty portraits, executed mainly in Ivry and right up to the last months before his death in March 1948, would henceforth constitute the main part of his graphic "oeuvre," established in 1986 by Paule Thévenin and Jacques Derrida in

Antonin Artaud: Dessins et portraits. Two works have been found since: *"La révolte des anges sortis des limbes"* [The revolt of the angels exited from limbo] and the *Portrait of Lily Dubuffet* [cat. nos. 22 and 54]. Works that have yet to be located are the portraits of Jean Dubuffet, Michel Tapié de Celeyran, Anne Manson, Alain Cuny, and Louis Broder, mentioned by Artaud in the different lists drawn up in preparation for the famous exhibition at the Galerie Pierre in July 1947.

He wanted the portraits shown as soon as possible to the Parisian public—along with the drawings of Rodez: did this mean that the portraits and the drawings had the same status and function? He insisted on explaining their oral and theatrical significance by a reading of texts *in situ*, and further clarified his intentions by writing "Le visage humain . . ." [The human face], which appeared in a catalogue prepared for this occasion.[2] Clearly the production of this autonomous work on large sheets of paper parallels (though in a different way than during the Rodez period) that done in the small schoolboy notebooks that he was never without, where the actual work of writing is done—extended, rather, since the projection of drawings is now preliminary to that of the writing that comes to surround or superimpose itself on them—in the same rhythm and creative spirit as the outpouring of pictograms: the boxes, nails, instruments of torture, shapeless graphic marks, parasitic and menacing figurines—his everyday "weapons"—tirelessly pound out, with an increasing and immediate effectiveness, the violent blows of expression in action, invading the pages here or there.

At first sight, none of this is present in the large drawings, which are done on sheets the same size as those of the Rodez drawings: these are actual portraits and self-portraits, in which

2
See pp. 94–97.

1
O.C. 1, 147–48.

the faces of his friends or people around him—
Roger Blin, Colette Thomas, Lily Dubuffet,
Jacques and Rolande Prevel, Arthur Adamov,
Marthe Robert, Michel de M'Uzan, the Pastier-
Thévenin family (Paule, Yves, Minouche,
Georges, and little Domnine), the Loebs (Pierre
and Edouard, the young Florence), Jacques
Germain, Mania Oïfer, Henri Pichette, Colette
Allendy, and so on—as well as his own, are
perfectly identifiable. Executed in front of the
model, in the pure classical tradition, duly signed
and dated, they seem entirely *deliberate* productions: apparently executed upon request
(occasioned by the fascinated desire of certain of
his intimates to be looked at by Artaud, perhaps
condemned and exposed by him?), given in
exchange for services rendered (drugs or treatments) or sold. Actually, what Artaud is doing in
these works, and through them—twenty-five
years after the first portraits and self-portraits of
the early 1920s—is interrogating the face to find
the hiding place of the *revolutionary* demand
"for a body not yet born" and to eject it from this
"empty force," this "field of death." He would
emphasize this in June 1947: "the human face is
temporarily, /and I say temporarily, /all that is
left of the demand, / of the *revolutionary*
demand of a body that is not yet and was never
in keeping with this face."3 The body, this gan-
gling puppet, without organs and without flesh,
this "machine of being" with its impossible
architecture, such as it appeared on what could
be considered anatomical plates drawn at Rodez,
thus disappears on the large sheets of Ivry, where
heads parade, brutally cut off at the neck: a necessary mutilation, a vital separation of head from
body, from a body not yet human, a shapeless
heap of suffering, a mass without organs, without *organization*. "My body is a real masonry of
posts, boxes, spikes, and nails,"4 and thus Artaud
attempts—only once, in the drawing *M. Victor*
[cat. no. 38]—to erect a *continuum*, to establish
an improbable equilibrium. We will have to
await the last drawings prior to his death to see,
constituted once again on the sheet of paper,
approximations of human torsos and corporal
architectures composed of a mass of heads.

A comparison with the early portraits of the

twenties (those of Dr. Dardel's young patient
"B.," of Edouard and Jeanne Toulouse, self-
portraits5)—sketched quickly but with respect
for "pure" drawing, where nevertheless a personal approach is already evident, seeking at the
outset to snare the secret and anxious part of the
self, the tension in the eyes, the grimaces of
expression—allow one to measure the accumu-
lated experience with which the author of the
"Theater of Cruelty" manifestos is endowed.
The man who resisted the physical and moral
misery of psychiatric confinement and electroshock treatment, who, as Paule Thévenin
tirelessly demonstrated, succeeded, through a
frenzied and *concerted* effort of breath, voice,
and gesture, in remaking a mental anatomy for
himself, possessed, after leaving Rodez, a total
mastery of his means of expression, oral and
graphic. And if for Artaud this mastery is necessarily communicated through "the pitiful
awkwardness of forms," it is an effective awkwardness, that of the fragmented drawings of
Rodez, so "sly/and so deft/that say SHIT to this
world." It was an astonishing graphic mastery
through which, finally, "the fullness of his dic-
tion is matched by the fullness of expression"6:
the *Portrait of Roger Blin* [cat. no. 39] stands out
in all respects as a "masterpiece" of a genre that
is no longer academic. Beyond the beautiful
evenness of the actor's own features, we see
re-presented the nervousness of the face, its
sensitivity and its vulnerablity, the acuity and
rebellious authority of the gaze; the hollows of
the bridge of the nose, the swollen eyelids, the
ruffled hair, the heaviness of the ears: sugges-
tions of the actor's destiny, the man's flaws, are
immediately brought to light by Artaud. We find
the same respect of individuality, the same intimate understanding, in the portraits of Rolande
Prevel and Florence Loeb [cat. nos. 34 and 40]:
the serene and luminous gentleness of the former is expressed in a curve of almost Matissean
sensuality, the restlessness of the adolescent in
heavy, dark lines. In the hypnotic *Self-Portrait*
of December 17, 1946 [cat. no. 41], the presence
of a lump of flesh isolated in the center of the
sheet—a sort of mask (or shroud) of painful
skin—appears as an obvious, natural given; the

5
Cf. *Antonin
Artaud: Oeuvres
sur papier*
(Marseille:
Musée Cantini,
1995),
cat. nos. 2–7.

6
O.C. 2, 172.

3
"Le Visage
humain"
(manu-
script version).

4
O.C. 14, bk. 2,
198.

gentleness of the delicate and skillful shading radiates in a halo the sadness of a gaze that has come from beyond time. Reproduced here, in its truth and humanity, is the accusatory presence of a living-dead man, his lips closed, but his throat constricted and his ears peeled.

Other graphic variations, in each case found and adapted to the distinctive features of others: hatched, messy strokes or a gnarled line tracing a sharp profile betray the inner torment of Jacques Prevel [cat. no. 48]; the purity of an oval contour expresses the ingenuousness of the little Domnine [cat. no. 42] or the "angelic" beauty of the actress Colette Thomas's face [cat. no. 49]: heads detached from their bodies and offered to the penetrating light of Artaud's gaze. Perhaps applicable here are the fascinated terms with which the director of *The Cenci* evoked the face of Iya Abdy as she was painted by Balthus, which he himself would make radiate in the role of Béatrice: "Balthus painted Iya Abdy as a primitive would have painted an angel: with the same skill, the same understanding of the spaces, lines, hollows, lights that make up space; and in Balthus's portrait, Iya Abdy is alive: she cries like a figure in relief appearing in a tale by Achim von Arnim. This is Iya Abdy's face, these are her hands that the light devours, but another being, who is Balthus, seems to be behind this face, and in this body, like a sorcerer who seduces a woman with his soul."[7]

Revealing remarks: something analogous will progressively appear in the portraits executed starting in April and May of 1947 (those of Jacques Prevel, Paule Thévenin, Mania Oïfer, Minouche Pastier, Michel de M'Uzan, Yves Thévenin, Jany de Ruy, et cetera), something that does in fact pertain to the theater, but to a theater of a cruelty "outside convention," the intimate terrain of which Artaud from now on finds on drawing paper. "What is truly theater is to make the sound erupt until the fiber of life is put on edge." Erected on the neck of the "shrieking lump," the heads isolated on the sheet as if to be better spotlit are no longer treated by Artaud in their objective truth, but brutalized, mistreated, nailed with signs, objects, and glossolalia: these isolate the face, place it "in

[7]
O.C. 5, 43–44.

relief," and inscribe it in a fully activated space occupied by written interjections that, in a way, hammer out the words of an extenuating *dialogue* established between him and the other, or conducted in the solitude of a recreated private conversation. The resonance of this exchange of "erupted" sounds can be both seen and heard: it is active, and Artaud is implementing here a process to ward off evil. By disclosing the secret of his friend's torment, in the *Portrait of Jacques Prevel* [cat. no. 44], Artaud seems to be protecting him from it or deflecting it from him with these inscriptions: "If Jacques Marie Prevel could know what Sin overwhelms him . . . may Jacques *Marie* Prevel not commit the Sin that his entire face meditates, may the Mary [Marie] within him premeditate against Jacques Prevel." These living heads "shriek," their mouths sewn shut, "like figures in relief" seen in a premonitory dream: hallucinating and hallucinatory visions, whose presence makes itself *felt* immediately. The rapid strokes of black pencil are mixed with graphic elements thrust in all directions, expanding them with thick color strokes (always those of fire: ocher, red, blue). The entire space of the paper becomes a responsive field traversed, attacked, until the "fiber of life is put on edge." All of this graphic and sonorous arrangement around the face indeed pertains to theater, an interior theater where a secret drama is now being played. It functions like a halo of cast shadow arranged to extend, to ink in (to anchor), to intensify the meaning of the gestures of the actors of the Alfred Jarry Theater such as Artaud conceived it in 1930. He repeated this in different terms in June 1947: "I am not yet sure of the limits at which the human body can stop." The graphic interjections of all sorts that encircle the portraits are there to imprison the human face with metal spikes and thus "nail down" its fate.

It is as if these heads "possessed" by Artaud, who seems to have placed himself "behind" them, are returned, *by him*, to their humanity, to the life of an "old human story" that was lost to view. Artaud returns insistently to his *power* to confront Medusa through these heads; he writes, in the text for the Galerie Pierre exhibition mentioned above, "The human face is an empty force, a field of death. . . . Which means that the human visage hasn't yet found its face and that it behooves the painter to find it in its place . . . For the human face, in fact, wears a perpetual death of sorts on its face, which it is incumbent on the painter precisely to save it from by restoring its own features. . . . wherefore in the portraits I have drawn have I avoided above all forgetting the nose the mouth the eyes the ears or the hair and strived to make the face that spoke to me tell the secret of an old human story." In a true act of cruelty, Artaud pits himself against man, summoning him to appear in the condition of his *becoming*, or in the condition of his *past*. At stake here for the model, as for himself, is a merciless revelation, a necessary exorcism of the "malediction" that weighs upon him. Manifested here, *beneath* the mask of the face drawn, carried, borne by him, is his own being strained by the frenzied will to un-make himself in order to re-make himself. On the *Portrait of Jany de Ruy* [cat. no. 56] he writes: "I am still terribly romantic like this drawing which represents me, in fact, too well, and I am weak, a *weakness*." As in the drawings of Rodez, the portraits retain the marks, the active traces, of his own battle with himself: "I have stippled and etched all the rages of my struggle, in view of a certain number of totems of being, and what is left are these miseries, my drawings."[8]

For Artaud, who placed these faces on the sheet, it was necessary, therefore, not only to mistreat what he calls the "subjectile"—the *inert* layer that is academic form, acquired language, the conventional strata that corset the mind—by imposing on it the probings of this projectile that is the writing and drawing pencil, but also to make this other, even more hateful subjectile that is the squalid human body "shriek" and thus to extract from it the truth of its "innate" being. "How? By an antilogical, antiphilosophical, anti-intellectual, anti*dialectical* blast of language through the pressure of my black pencil and that's all."[9] Guided by him, this is an act of rebirth, a demand for birth, "the attempt to arrive at the horizon of an open infinite." The deep significance and the function of these portraits are thus of the most profound conse-

quence and—Artaud threateningly alerts us—it is out of the question to consider them "works of esthetic simulation of reality." Again in "Le visage humain . . ." he writes: "None of them strictly speaking are works. All of them are drafts, I mean probings or burrowings in all the directions of chance, possibility, luck, or destiny. I have not sought to refine my strokes or my effects, but to manifest some sorts of linear patent truths." The portraits drawn by Artaud are not of any particular esthetic category— they are *without style*; instead they pertain to a metaphysics of the tangible and of the evident.

As re-presentations of the "human" face revealed in its truth, as manifestations, demands, and again conjurations, the portraits indeed have the same status as the drawings of Rodez and the first "spells," the missives, burnt, stained, and riddled with holes, of the years 1937–39. They act as vehicles for magical effects; like the *Portrait of Henri Pichette* [cat. no. 60], called a "gris-gris" by Artaud, they constitute exorcisms of curses, as Artaud wrote in February 1947, bodily vituperations "against the exigencies of spatial form, of perspective, of measure, of equilibrium, of dimension and, via this vituperative act of protest, a condemning of the psychic world which, like a crab louse, digs its way into the physical, and, like an incubus or succubus, claims to have given it shape." Artaud, fascinated by van Gogh's convulsive self portraits, in which he sees reflected his own struggle and his own destiny, then writes, that same month, *Van Gogh, the Man Suicided by Society*.

In the last large drawings before his death, dated December 1947 and January 1948, the evocations of heads—essentially faces of women "possessed," loved and lost, that he refers to as his "daughters of an awakening heart"—are multiplied, piled up, or superimposed on the same sheet of paper, forming sorts of human trunks—"trumeaux" (shanks) as Artaud calls them—protective fetishes that recall (though Artaud wouldn't have known this) the totems of New Ireland. By linking them together—the pencil traces between them a feverish network sweeping across the space, constituting the tight web of a membrane made to snare them—

8
O.C. 21, 266–67.

9
Luna Park, no. 5
(October 1979).

Artaud seems to be attempting in a final moment to portray a cluster of body fragments already wasted by death: as if, by this multiple proliferation filling the space with a "corpus" of lines, he could effect a transsubstantiation of the shattered, residual debris of his own body waiting to be born. The December 1947 *Self-Portrait* [cat. no. 64], his last (which he dated December 1948, after his death), eludes, even more than the others, all descriptive function. Out of an assemblage of corporal fragments there seems to be constituted, in an almost triumphal and theatrical effigy, what could be the emblematic bust— one could almost say the glorious body—of Antonin Artaud; the habitual severed head—or rather the poet's mask of taut skin and his strangely oblique gaze upon which our own gaze is skewered—sits atop an unlikely combination of head, hand, ear, totem: his large hand, gnarled, nervous, and alive, the severed ear (like van Gogh's), his own head already dead ("the head that oppresses me," he had said to Thévenin) and, at the center, what could be a spinal column, the collapse of a "totem of being": scattered, ridiculous trophies, arranged in an arc like armor, *disjuncta membra* which, from the beginning, constitute the "beingness" of Artaud. Metallic, glittering bursts of graphite pencil, which sweep the space with sharp scratches like the slashes of a knife, incise the sheet with a tangle of features by turns swift and crushed with heavy punctuations or more sensitive shadings, the energy truly resonating—

here scraping, there modulated—and what is released from this orchestration reflects a full-blown joust, in which gesture and breath, cry and whistling participate more than ever. The drawn sheet itself becomes a sort of breastplate, armor against the invading forces of that "subjectile" which Artaud did not cease to combat.

Antonin Artaud's portraits, the exercises of cruelty that he bequeathed us, speak to us, stare at us: in turn they impose upon the viewer an implacable mirrored reflection, forcing him to look hard at what can not be envisaged: to understand, perhaps, that man is only a man when he becomes the monster of his suffering. They also allow one to *en-visage*—to invest this place where it has taken refuge—the inner anarchy of a body without organs, this field laid open to the forces of life and death, traversed by circuits, fluxes, connections, riddled with indelible flaws; the drawing of Antonin Artaud is no longer anything but the image or memory of this body, or rather of this "machine that has breath" searching "for a world that is lost and that no human language includes"; it is, Artaud informs us, "no more itself than a tracing, a sort of reduced copy."[10] Nevertheless, what he considers a copy has the irremediable "force of an explosive rocket, like the beating of a shattered heart." It possesses in our eyes the impact of an indestructible and natural reality, in the instant of a gaze that melts us.

Translated by Jeanine Herman

10
Luna Park, no. 5
(October 1979).

"Le visage humain…"

ANTONIN ARTAUD : JUNE 1947

The human face
is an empty force, a
field of death.
The old revolutionary
demand for a form
that has never corres-
ponded to its body, that started
off as something other
than the body.
Thus is it absurd
to denounce the academicism
of a painter
who currently
persists in reproducing
the features of the human face
such as they are; for such
as they are they have not
yet found the form that they
promise and designate;
and do better than outlining
pounding away at it
from morning to night,
and in the midst of ten thousand dreams,
as in the crucible of a passional
palpitation never wearied.
Which means
that the human visage
hasn't yet found its face
and that it behooves the painter
to find it in its place.
Which means however
that the human visage
such as it is still looks
for itself with two eyes a
nose a mouth
and the two auricular
cavities
which answer the holes
of the orbits as
the four openings

Le visage humain
est une force vide, un
champ de mort.
La vieille revendication
révolutionnaire d'une forme
qui n'a jamais corres-
pondu à son corps, qui partait
pour être autre chose
que le corps.
C'est ainsi qu'il est absurde
de reprocher d'être académique
à un peintre
qui à l'heure qu'il est
s'obstine encore à reproduire
les traits du visage humain
tels qu'ils sont; car tels
qu'ils sont ils n'ont pas
encore trouvé la forme qu'ils
indiquent et désignent;
et font plus que d'esquisser
mais du matin au soir,
et au milieu de dix mille rêves,
pilonnent comme dans le
creuset d'une palpitation
passionnelle jamais lassée.
Ce qui veut dire
que le visage humain
n'a pas encore trouvé sa façe
et que c'est au peintre
à la lui donner.
Mais ce qui veut dire
que la face humaine
telle qu'elle est se cherche
encore avec deux yeux un
nez une bouche
et les deux cavités
auriculaires
qui répondent aux trous
des orbites comme
les quatre ouvertures

of the burial chamber of the
impending death.
For the human face,
in fact, wears
a perpetual death of sorts
on its face
which it is incumbent on the painter precisely
to save it from
by restoring
its own features.
For thousands and thousands of years indeed,
the human face has talked
and breathed
and one is under the impression still
that it has not begun to
say what it is and what it knows.
Not a single painter in
the history of art, from Holbein
to Ingres, whom I know of
has succeeded in making it talk,
this face of man. Holbein's portraits
or those of Ingres are but
thick walls that explain
nothing of the ancient mortal architecture
that buttresses the
arches of eyelids
or tails into
the cylindrical tunnel
of the two mural
cavities of the ears.
Van Gogh only
could make of the human
head a portrait
which was the
bursting flare of a
throbbing,
exploded heart.
His own.
Van Gogh's head with
a felt hat
renders null and void
all the attempts at abstract
painting which can be
made after him, until the
end of all eternities.
For this face of a butcher
greedy, projected as though
fired from a cannon, upon

du caveau de la
prochaine mort.
Le visage humain
porte en effet une espèce
de mort perpétuelle
sur son visage
dont c'est au peintre justement
à le sauver
en lui rendant
ses propres traits.
Depuis mille et mille ans en effet
que le visage humain parle
et respire
on a encore comme l'impression
qu'il n'a pas encore commencé à
dire ce qu'il est et ce qu'il sait
et je ne connais pas un peintre dans
l'histoire de l'art, d'Holbein
à Ingres qui, ce visage
d'homme, soit parvenu à
le faire parler. Les portraits
d'Holbein ou d'Ingres sont des
murs épais, qui n'expliquent
rien de l'antique architecture mortelle
qui s'arc-boute sous les
arcs de voûte des paupières
ou s'encastre
dans le tunnel cylindrique
des deux cavités
murales des oreilles.
Le seul van Gogh
a su tirer d'une tête
humaine un portrait
qui soit la
fusée explosive du
battement d'un coeur
éclaté.
Le sien.
La tête de van Gogh au
chapeau mou rend nulles
et non avenues
toutes les tentatives de peintures
abstraites qui pourront être
faites depuis lui, jusqu'à la
fin des éternités.
Car ce visage de boucher
avide, projeté comme
en coup de canon à la surface

the most extreme surface of the canvas
and which is suddenly
stopped
by a glassy eye
staring inwards
exhausts the totality of
the most specious
secrets of the abstract world
in which nonfigurative painting
may take pleasure,
wherefore in
the portraits I have drawn
have I avoided above all
forgetting the nose the mouth
the eyes the ears or
the hair and strived
to make the
face that spoke to me
tell the secret
of an old
human story that
has passed as dead in
the heads
of Ingres or Holbein.
I have at times gathered
next to the human heads
objects trees
or animals because
I haven't yet ascertained
the limits within which
the body of the human
ego can stop.
I have moreover definitely
done away with art
style or talent in
all the drawings
you will see here. I mean to say
that woe unto who
would consider them as
works of art,
works of aesthetic
simulation of reality.
None of them strictly
speaking are
works.
All of them are drafts,
I mean
probings or

la plus extrême de la toile
et qui tout d'un coup se
voit arrêté
par un oeil vide,
et retourné vers le dedans,
épuise à fond tous
les secrets les plus
spécieux du monde abstrait
où la peinture non figurative
peut se complaire,
c'est pourquoi dans
les portraits que j'ai dessinés,
j'ai évité avant tout
d'oublier le nez la bouche
les yeux les oreilles ou
les cheveux, mais j'ai cherché
à faire dire au
visage qui me parlait
le secret
d'une vieille histoire
humaine qui a
passé comme morte dans
les têtes
d'Ingres ou d'Holbein.
J'ai fait venir parfois
à côté des têtes humaines
des objets des arbres
ou des animaux parce que
je ne suis pas encore sûr
des limites auxquelles le
corps du moi
humain peut s'arrêter.
J'en ai d'ailleurs définitivement
brisé avec l'art
le style ou le talent dans
tous les dessins que l'on
verra ici. Je veux dire
que malheur à qui
les considérerait comme
des oeuvres d'art,
des oeuvres de simulation
esthétique de la réalité.
Aucun n'est à
proprement parler une
oeuvre.
Tous sont des ébauches,
je veux dire
des coups de sonde ou

burrowings
in all the directions
of chance, possibi-
lity, luck, or
destiny.
I have not sought
to refine my strokes
or my effects,
but to manifest
some sorts of
linear patent truths
whose value would reside
as well in words,
written sentences,
as in graphic expression
and linear perspective.
So it is that several drawings
are mixtures of poems and
portraits
of written interjections
and plastic evocations
of elements taken from
the materials
of human or animal forms.
So it is that
these drawings must be accepted
in the barbarity and disorder
of their
graphic expression "which never
concerned itself with
art" but with the sincerity
and spontaneity
of the stroke.

Text for the catalogue of the exhibition
Portraits et dessins par Antonin Artaud,
Galerie Pierre, Paris, 4-20 July 1947

Translated by Roger McKeon

de butoir donnés
dans tous les sens
du hasard, de la possibi-
lité, de la chance, ou de
la destinée.
Je n'ai pas cherché
à y soigner mes traits
ou mes effets,
mais à y manifester des
sortes de vérités
linéaires patentes qui
vaillent aussi
bien par les mots,
les phrases écrites
que le graphisme
et la perspective des traits.
C'est ainsi que plusieurs dessins
sont des mélanges de poèmes et de
portraits
d'interjections écrites
et d'évocations plas-
tiques d'éléments de
matériaux de personnages
d'homme ou d'animaux.
C'est ainsi qu'il faut accepter
ces dessins dans la
barbarie et le désordre
de leur
graphisme "qui ne s'est
jamais préoccupé de
l'art" mais de la sincérité
et de la spontanéité
du trait.

34
Portrait of Rolande Prevel
20 August 1946
Graphite
10½ x 8⅝" (27 x 22 cm)
Musée Cantini, Marseille

27 d'août 1946   antonin Artaud

35
Portrait of Jacques Prevel
27 August 1946
Graphite
11 x 8⅞" (28 x 22.5 cm)
Musée Cantini, Marseille

36
Portrait of Pierre Loeb
6 October 1946
Graphite
10 ½ x 8 ⅛" (27 x 20 cm)
Collection Florence Loeb

37
Portrait of Sima Feder
7 October 1946
Graphite
24⅞ x 18⅞" (63 x 48 cm)
Collection Florence Loeb

aritovru artour
7 octobre 1946

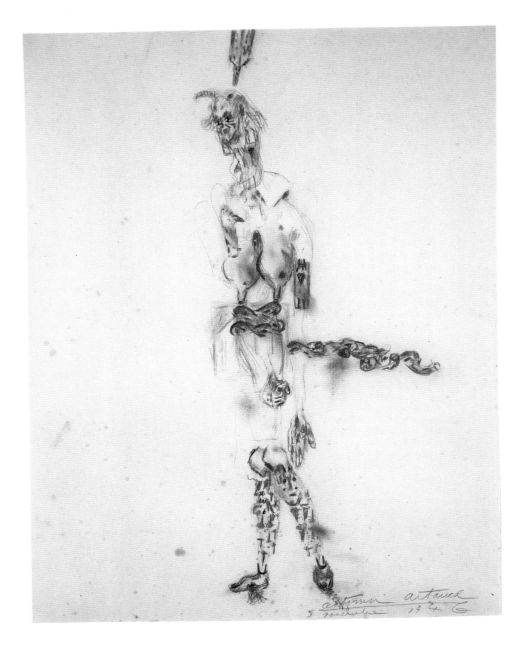

38
M. Victor
5 November 1946
Graphite
25¼ x 19½" (64 x 49 cm)
Private collection

39
Portrait of Roger Blin
22 November 1946
Graphite
29 x 20⅞" (74 x 53 cm)
Musée National d'Art
Moderne—Centre de Création
Industrielle, Centre Georges
Pompidou, Paris. Bequest of
Paule Thévenin, 1993

antoine detaer

22 novembre 1946

40
Portrait of Florence Loeb
4 December 1946
Graphite
26⅝ x 20⅞" (68 x 53 cm)
Collection Florence Loeb

41
Self-Portrait
17 December 1946
Graphite
24¾ x 18⅛" (62 x 46 cm)
Collection Florence Loeb

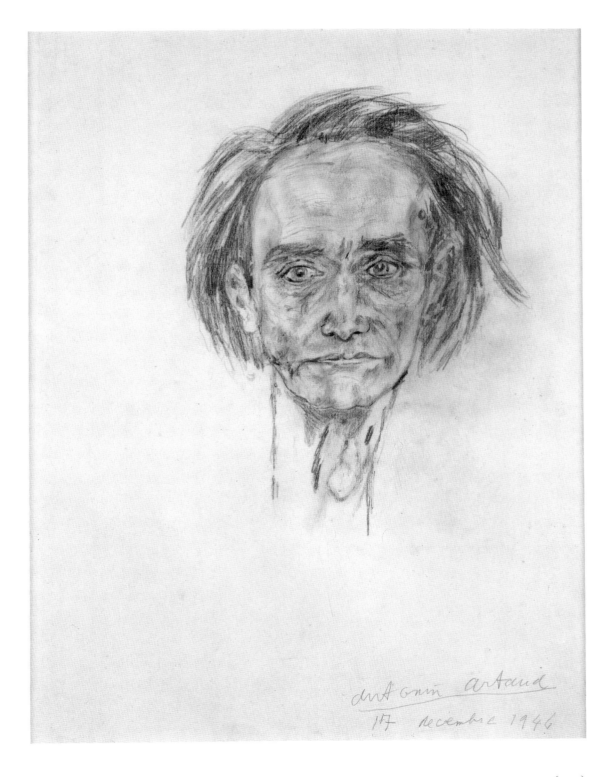

42
Portrait of Domnine Thévenin
7 March 1947
Graphite
25½ x 20⅞" (65 x 53 cm)
Paris. Bequest of Paule
Thévenin, 1993

43
Portrait of Marcel Bisiaux
25 April 1947
Graphite
22 x 17¼" (56 x 44 cm)
Private collection

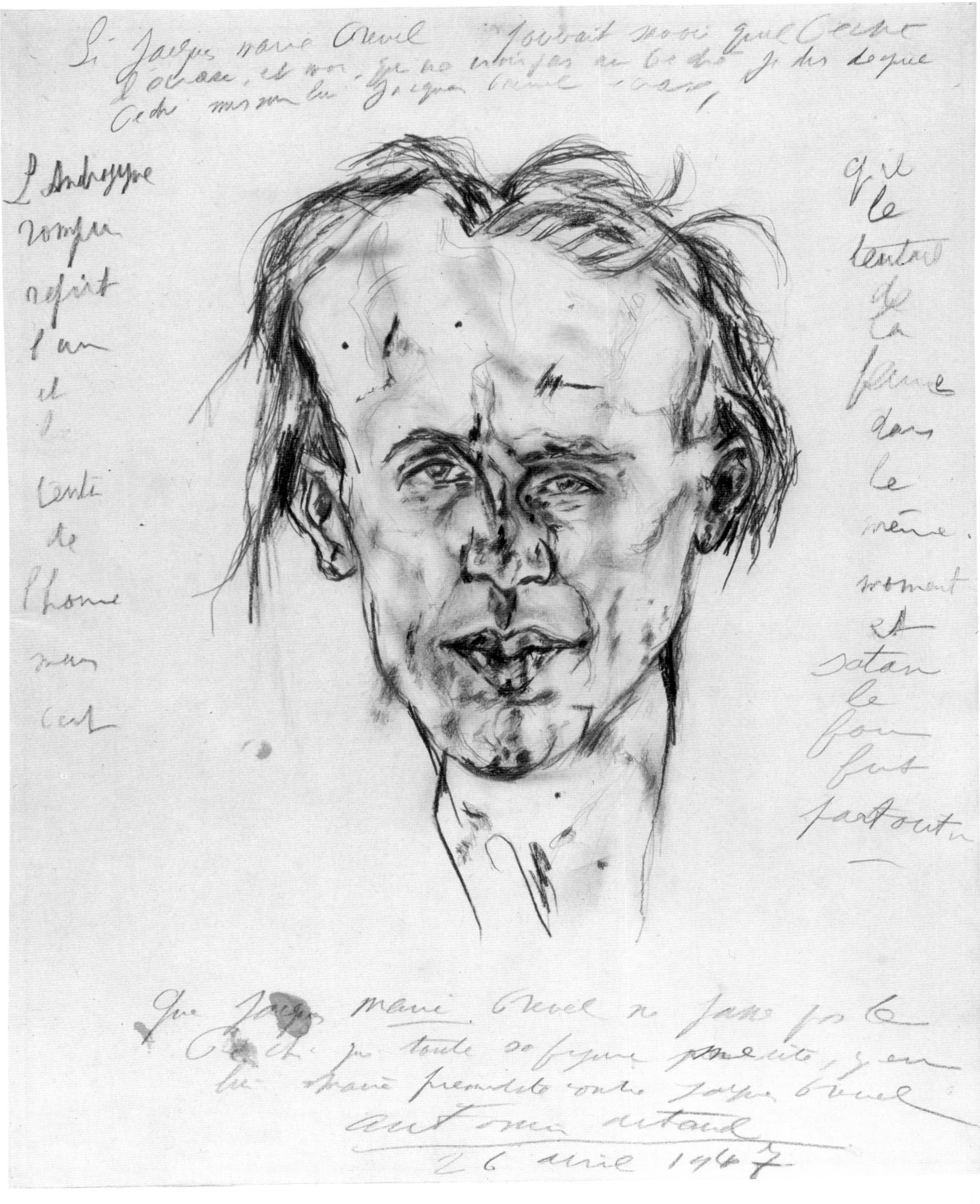

Si Jacques Marie Revel pouvait savoir que c'est
d'abord, et moi, que ne croyais pas ... je dis depuis
ce dit ... le Jacques Revel ...

L'androgyne
rompu
reprit
l'un
et
l'
tenté
de
l'homme
nous
cela

qu'il
le
tentant
de
la
femme
dans
le
même
moment
et
satan
le
fou
fut
partout
—

Que Jacques Marie Revel ne fasse pas ce
... je toute sa figure ..., je en
... Marie première contre Jacques Revel
antonin artaud
26 avril 1947

45
Portrait of Paule Thévenin
27 April 1947
Graphite
28¾ x 21" (73 x 53 cm)
Musée National d'Art Moderne—
Centre de Création Industrielle,
Centre Georges Pompidou, Paris.
Bequest of Paule Thévenin, 1993

44
Portrait of Jacques Prevel
26 April 1947
Graphite
25 x 19⅛" (63.5 x 48.5 cm)
Musée National d'Art
Moderne—Centre de
Création Industrielle,
Centre Georges Pompidou,
Paris

46
Portrait of Minouche Pastier
May 1947
Graphite
29¼ x 20½" (74.5 x 52 cm)
Musée National d'Art
Moderne—Centre de Création
Industrielle, Centre Georges
Pompidou, Paris. Bequest of
Paule Thévenin, 1993

47
Portrait of Mania Oïfer
May 1947
Graphite
25¼ x 20⅞" (64 x 53 cm)
Musée Cantini, Marseille

Antonin Artaud
mai 1947

48
Portrait of Jacques Prevel in
Profile
11 May 1947
Graphite
22 1/8 x 17 5/8" (56.5 x 45 cm)
Musée Cantini, Marseille

49
Portrait of Colette Thomas
21 May 1947
Graphite
25½ x 19⅝" (65 x 50 cm)
Private collection

antonin artaud
22 mai 1947

51
Portrait of Paule Thévenin
or *Paule with Irons*
(*Paule aux ferrets*)
24 May 1947
Graphite and wax crayon
25¼ x 20¾" (64 x 52.5 cm)
Musée National d'Art Moderne—
Centre de Création Industrielle,
Centre Georges Pompidou, Paris.
Bequest of Paule Thévenin, 1993

50
Portrait of Minouche Pastier
22 May 1947
Graphite and wax crayon
25 x 18⅞" (63.5 x 47.8 cm)
Musée National d'Art
Moderne—Centre de Création
Industrielle, Centre Georges
Pompidou, Paris

arthur adamov
auteur

d'avoir
écrit   unique
dans   l'histoire
des   lettres
                    antonin artaud

52
Portrait of Arthur Adamov
c. 17 June 1947
Graphite and wax crayon
26½ x 21½" (67 x 54 cm)
Collection Florence Loeb

53
Portrait of a Man
c. 20 June 1947
Graphite and wax crayon
24 x 18⅞" (61 x 48 cm)
Private collection

54
Portrait of Lily Dubuffet
22 June 1947
Graphite and wax crayon
26¼ x 19¼" (67 x 49 cm)
Private collection

55
Portrait of Yves Thévenin
24 June 1947
Graphite and wax crayon
25 ½ x 19 ¾" (65 x 50 cm)
Musée National d'Art Moderne—
Centre de Création Industrielle,
Centre Georges Pompidou, Paris.
Bequest of Paule Thévenin, 1993

voi un · · ·
dessin aujourd'hui
qui dira
outrepasse que
d de Saint
loin antonin

Leonard
de Vinci

il en est
pas surtout par
le demin par le
fait de l'autr
encore trop

des rides ·········· enfants
de rides jaunes, et je les envoie com-
battre dans mon corps — seulement
je manque d'énergie et cela
se voit, et je suis encore
terriblement romantique
comme ce dessin qui me
représente, en fait, trop bien,
et je suis faible une faiblesse

Antonin Artaud
juillet 1947

56
Portrait of Jany de Ruy
2 July 1947
Graphite and wax crayon
25½ x 19⅝" (65 x 50 cm)
Musée National d'Art Moderne—
Centre de Création Industrielle,
Centre Georges Pompidou, Paris

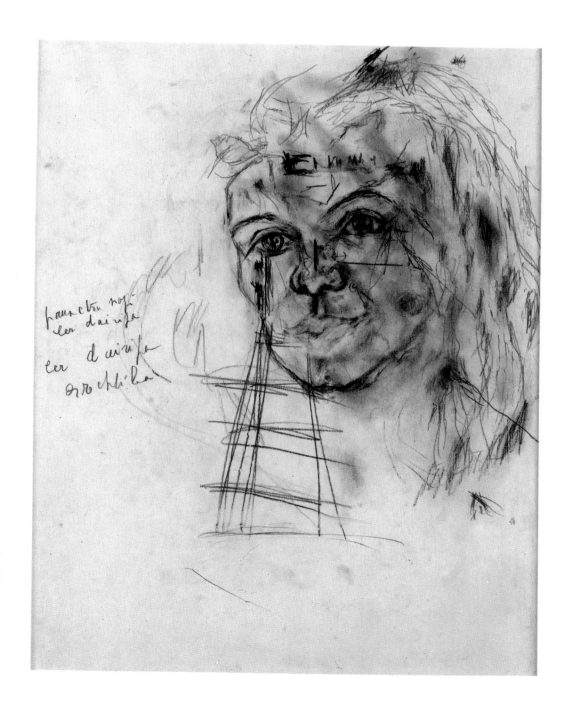

57
Portrait of Colette Thomas
c. August 1947
Graphite
23¼ x 17⅝" (59 x 45 cm)
Musée National d'Art Moderne—
Centre de Création Industrielle,
Centre Georges Pompidou, Paris.
Bequest of Paule Thévenin, 1993

58
Portrait of Colette Allendy
25 August 1947
Graphite and wax crayon
25½ x 19⅝" (65 x 50 cm)
Musée National d'Art
Moderne—Centre de
Création Industrielle,
Centre Georges Pompidou,
Paris. Bequest of Paule
Thévenin, 1993

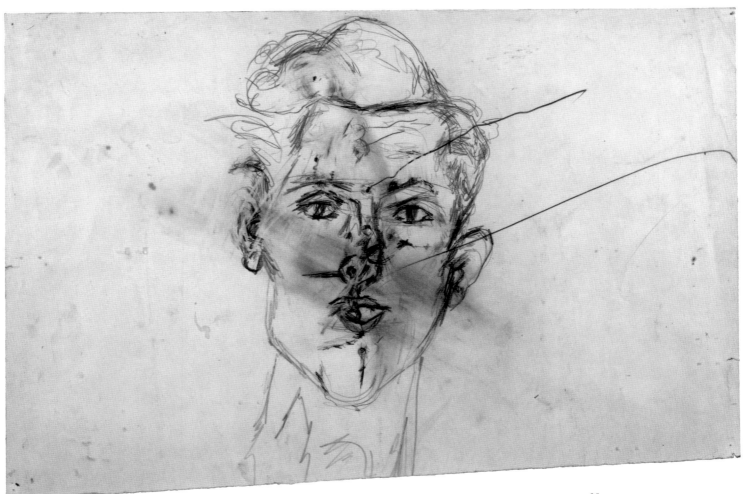

59
Portrait of Alain Gheerbrant
c. November 1947
Graphite
13⅞ x 19⅞" (34.8 [left side],
32.4 cm [right side] x 50.3 cm)
Private collection

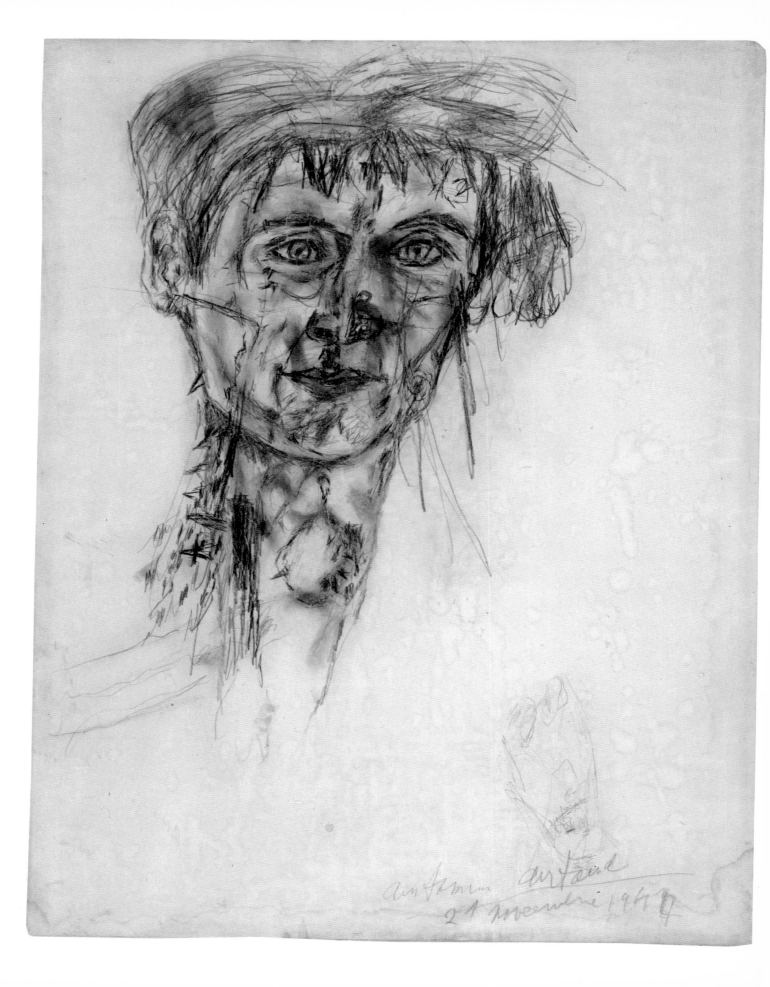

Antonin Artaud
21 novembre 1947

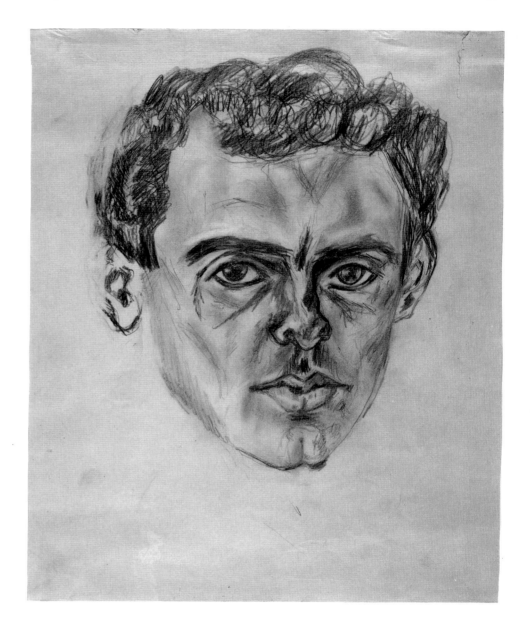

61
Portrait of Georges Pastier
December 1947
Graphite
17⅝ x 13¾" (45 x 35 cm)
Musée National d'Art Moderne—
Centre de Création Industrielle,
Centre Georges Pompidou, Paris.
Bequest of Paule Thévenin, 1993

60
Portrait of Henri Pichette
or *Gris-gris*
21 November 1947
Graphite
25¼ x 19¾" (64.7 x 49.8 cm)
Musée National d'Art Moderne—
Centre de Création Industrielle,
Centre Georges Pompidou, Paris

63
Faces
c. December 1947
Graphite
25¼ x 20⅛" (64 x 51 cm)
Collection Florence Loeb

62
Self-Portrait
c. December 1947
Graphite
14½ x 10½" (37 x 27 cm)
Collection Florence Loeb

64
Self-Portrait
December 1947
Graphite
25½ x 19⅝" (65 x 50 cm)
Musée National d'Art Moderne—
Centre de Création Industrielle,
Centre Georges Pompidou, Paris.
Bequest of Paule Thévenin, 1993

65
The Projection of the True Body
(*La Projection du véritable corps*)
18 November 1946–December 1947
or January 1948
Graphite and wax crayon
21¼ x 29½" (54 x 75 cm)
Musée National d'Art Moderne—
Centre de Création Industrielle,
Centre Georges Pompidou, Paris.
Bequest of Paule Thévenin, 1993

66
Untitled
c. January 1948
Graphite
25½ x 19⅝" (65 x 50 cm)
Musée National d'Art
Moderne—Centre de
Création Industrielle, Centre
Georges Pompidou, Paris.
Bequest of Paule Thévenin,
1993

67
Untitled
c. January 1948
Graphite
25½ x 19⅝" (65 x 50 cm)
Musée National d'Art
Moderne—Centre de
Création Industrielle, Centre
Georges Pompidou, Paris.
Bequest of Paule Thévenin,
1993

68
Untitled
c. February 1948
Graphite
25½ x 19⅝" (65 x 50 cm)
Musée National d'Art Moderne—
Centre de Création Industrielle,
Centre Georges Pompidou, Paris.
Bequest of Paule Thévenin, 1993

Antonin Artaud, 1947. Photographed by Georges Pastier.

CONTEMPORARY RESPONSES TO ARTAUD

On the following pages are interviews with three contemporary artists whose work reflects, directly or indirectly, the influence of Antonin Artaud's thought and art. The interviews were conducted by Margit Rowell and Sylvère Lotringer.

Nancy Spero
"avec quels impossibles . . ."
from the Artaud Paintings
1970
Cut-and-pasted papers, gouache, and ink
25 x 19¾" (63.5 x 50.4 cm)
Private collection

A Conversation with Nancy Spero

Margit Rowell and Sylvère Lotringer

Nancy Spero and her husband the painter Leon Golub lived in Paris from 1959 to 1964 and, after returning to the United States, settled in New York. In 1969 and 1970 Spero made a series of works on paper that she calls the Artaud Paintings, *which were inspired by the writings of Artaud. The works were exhibited once, in 1971, but then not shown publicly again until 1980. They have since been recognized, together with the* Codex Artaud *series that followed, as key elements in her body of work.*

SYLVÈRE LOTRINGER: You said that even before you read the City Lights anthology,* you already knew of Artaud. How did you hear of him?

NANCY SPERO: I can't be precise—probably during the Paris years.

SL: Did you read him in French at the time?

NS: No. I was doing the *War Series* at that time, in the sixties. We had come back to the United States, after five years in France, at the end of 1964, and the Vietnam War was going on. I wanted to make manifestos in response to the war, antiwar work, but I didn't want to use the usual propagandistic means. I equated the violence of war with violent imagery. Violent sexual imagery was the most offensive and angry means to challenge the yes-saying of conventional pro-war pieties. This was in early 1966, making the transition from the Paris Black Paintings, the somber elegiac existential paintings that I had been working on for five years.

MARGIT ROWELL: With an Artaud inspiration, or not yet?

NS: No, not yet. It must have been the summer of '69— I was doing the *War Series*—I bought the Artaud anthology and took it to Puerto Rico—we used to go with the kids, it was very inexpensive then. Our middle son, Philip, started translating the anthology back into French. And I said, That's it, this complaint of Artaud's is the direct way to go from the violence of the war to the violence of the exposed self. Artaud screaming and yelling, hysterical about the silencing, the castration of the tongue. And I said, That's me, you know? That's myself, the artist, a woman artist. I didn't quite zero in on it, but I knew it was about being a woman artist. So for the next two years I continued the *War Series* but shifted imagery to the self-recognitions that became the Artaud Paintings.

What I would do is stockpile images. I was working exclusively on paper; part of my resistance as an artist in the *War Series* was a decision not to work any more on

* Jack Hirschman, ed., *Antonin Artaud: An Anthology* (San Francisco: City Lights, 1965).

canvas. I shifted completely to work on paper. Big canvases carried the male look! The "establishment"! No one was paying attention. I was madder than hell about the war. I figured out later on that probably since I had three small sons, I wouldn't want my sons going off to war, the raging Vietnam War I considered an abomination. So the *War Series* was like an exorcism. And perhaps the Artaud series as well. Artaud's terrible sense of disappointment, in his fantastic letters to Jacques Rivière when he was a young writer, moved me. I knew enough French to realize that Artaud was classically trained and brilliant, and that he was tearing away at the fabric of structure and language, railing against society and the shunting aside of the artist. More than thirty years later his voice still challenges me, his calls for justice.

To get back to the Artaud Paintings, the writing on them is in English for most of the first year, 1969. Then I decided that as brilliant as some of these translations were, I would go to the French, to Artaud's direct voice. I fractured his already fractured screams and hysteria; I took great liberties. I acknowledge he would have disapproved, even hated what I was doing, using and disrupting his language for my purposes. That's why I wrote/painted this letter to him in 1969.

SL: What was the letter?

NS: "Artaud, I could not have borne to know you alive, your despair. Spero." In the *Codex Artaud* series I continued imagistically from the *War Series*. Artaud became my great collaborator, the presence in the studio. I began to use Japanese rice paper. I couldn't paint and scumble on it the same way I had with other papers. I painted on it directly and started collaging. I'd tear and repair paper. I also wrote with my left hand while I scavenged irregularly through the writings, cutting images and language, collaging, recombining, tearing, and so on.

SL: So then you were aware of the fact that your relationship with Artaud was slanted?

NS: Of course! He would have hated my process. But perhaps as a presence in my studio, he might have recognized what was in common between us. This might be too self-serving! In any case, he was a misogynist.

SL: Was he really a misogynist?

NS: Yes! Maybe it is just that he was so irritated and so ill and everything, although there is his extraordinary hallucinatory evocation of feminine body language. "I feel the Church between my thighs, moaning, holding

SL: At the same time, he created a circle of women around him, like benefactors, women who had been good to him. I think to him women were sacred: they were both abominable and extremely desirable.

NS: But he suffered from the self-imposed denial of his own sexuality.

SL: So his misogyny is not some kind of cynicism towards women; he needed women, he was totally enthralled by women. It is their sexuality he found threatening. He equated them with sexuality. And so I wanted to suggest that you reappropriated his misogyny and turned it into something else, you got the anger out of him and reused it for your own needs.

NS: For all his "presence" in my work, the misunderstandings, the tensions of our differences have to be vast.

SL: And his anger towards God; I don't think you share that.

NS: If there is a God—

SL: Artaud was angry at society because God created it that way, he was angry at sexuality and gender because He made it such that people would be captured by it. So like a disk jockey, you lifted out of Artaud the refrain that you needed, right?

NS: Yes. Actually, there is a piece in my *Torture of Women* series in which he talked about all his imagined daughters, and there's another quote: "I saw the corpse of my daughter Annie incinerated, and her sexual organs squandered and divided after her death by the police of France."* I reincorporated Artaud.

SL: So Artaud bled all over the *Torture*.

NS: Right.

SL: And you didn't feel uncomfortable with this aspect? You know, finally Artaud saw women either as virgins or as whores, the traditional dichotomy. But he was far worse, more extreme than most.

NS: Among my "company" of actors, I do evoke images of goddesses. At a mythical level goddesses have many seemingly contradictory guises, human aspects, but writ large, devouring and protective. Sheela na-gig is a goddess of fertility and destruction, birth and death. She spreads an enormous vulva . . . or Artemis as healer and destroyer, interwoven in multiple layers. Artaud: Woman as whore. Dare I say, he screams in his partial guise as a woman?

MR: And how did you switch from the small paintings to the *Codex*?

SL: Is there anything else we should know about the small paintings before we switch over to the *Codex*?

NS: The quotes in the Artaud Paintings are briefer, more succinct, less fractured than the *Codex*.

SL: Was there any logic in the sequence of the Artaud Paintings?

NS: No. It's a "logic" of contradiction, refusal, fracture.

SL: But they are fairly different from one another. Some of them are geometric—

* *Torture of Women* series (1976), detail, panel 7.

NS: I take from wherever—yes, geometry, but also Egyptian art, the Bayeux tapestry, yoga figures, roller skaters, and so on. I was not unaware that conceptual art was going on, but I did it in my fashion, you see? It did not match what was going on. My sources and philosophy are different. Geometry? Sure. Is Tantric art geometric? Or outsider art? I deny a significant "New York" abstract or conceptual input.

SL: The idea of the collage came from the *War Series*?

NS: Yes. But previously, even in art school days, I had done torn collage on paper and I had done writing on paper and canvas intermittently during my whole career as an artist, although not to the extent of the *Codex* or the 1970s work. I used a great deal of language on the subject of the status of women.

SL: But the language at that point with Artaud was not informative, it was very emotional and expressionistic.

NS: It was angry. The *War Series* and the Artaud work are very angry.

MR: So in fact, you met Artaud and he was a kind of a vehicle for what you were already trying to express.

NS: Exactly.

SL: You hijacked him.

NS: I hijacked him. And at the time, a critic said that the *Codex* pieces looked like huge blackmail notes. Angry letters to the world. I joined Artaud in his assault. Figures are sexualized and enigmatic, often androgynous, tongues are sticking out all over the place—defiant, phallic tongues.

SL: The tongue thing is both phallic and castrating, or castrated. It's wholly ambivalent and reversible. Did you get that from Uccello? Remember Artaud's phrase, "Leave your tongue, Paolo Uccello, leave your tongue . . . I tear out my tongue"?

NS: That's interesting; Leon wrote an essay in the late fifties, never published, in which he compared [Picasso's] *Guernica* to the Beatus illuminations of the Apocalypse. We pored over this book, this beautiful, fantastic, ferocious Apocalypse, with animals drowning, their tongues extended. I had tongues sticking out in the late fifties works, the "fuck you" paintings, predecessors of the *War Series* and Artaud. I was so far out I considered myself in the underground's underground. I was totally out of the loop and angry. I had become a member in the late 1960s of women's action and discussion groups in the arts, offshoots of the Art Workers' Coalition: W.A.R. [Women Artists in Revolution] and the Ad Hoc Committee of Women Artists in which we investigated women's status in the world and women artists. This gave me empirical data for my work. It was rather fun to go to the director of The Museum of Modern Art and say, "We want parity," and demand it: "Listen to what we're saying!" And to investigate and picket the Whitney Museum.

MR: How long did it take you to exhibit in New York after you came back from Paris?

NS: We came back in '64, and the only occasions I showed were in antiwar shows. In the late sixties I and five other women artists organized A.I.R. Gallery. That's where I first showed *Codex Artaud* and subsequently *Torture of Women.*

MR: When did the *Codex* start?

NS: 1971. I worked on the *Codex* for two years.

MR: Was this immediately after the Artaud Paintings? Was there anything else in between?

NS: I worked on the Artaud Paintings for two years, 1969 and 1970. There was nothing in between. I had been doing small works for all these years. The works in the *War Series* were about thirty-six by twenty-four inches; the Artaud Paintings were twenty-five by nineteen inches, more or less. I decided to work larger. I briefly tried oil painting again. It didn't work out. I hated it. Then I took pieces of archival art paper I had around the studio and began piecing them together. The first *Codex* is assembled paper and disparate images in tension with Artaud's fractured texts in bulletin type, and the works in the *Codex Artaud* series range in size from eighteen inches by four feet to twenty-five inches by twenty-five feet. I gave myself leeway.

SL: Most people want to become Artaud, but you wanted Artaud to become you.

NS: Not really. I was very moved, but on the other hand, I didn't want to get over-involved with his obsessions. It was very important to relate to Artaud and yet retain autonomy.

SL: This kind of possibility of moving in the big scrolls, of doing movement, also freed you somehow from Artaud.

NS: Very much, and it freed me from the conventional respect for the rectangle of paintings, a rebellion against painting on canvas as well as an angry defiance of art systems and expectations. An extended linear format: I thought this work can never be framed. Who would buy it? I was into the antiwar thing, and then the women artist protests or the Art Workers' Coalition. It didn't occur to me that I would even enter the system, although I was anxious to have a dialogue with the art world.

SL: That's something you had in common with Artaud. Artaud thought "all writing is pig shit," yet he wrote. He was very aware of that.

NS: Of course. One wants to enter the system; one can't be totally out of it. *Torture of Women* is twenty inches high by 125 feet long. When I showed it in A.I.R., a woman facetiously said, If I bought this piece, where would I put it in my home? I thought, That's the way it is. Dealers are going to be facetious about this. How could it be feasible? The same for the Artaud works.

SL: Did you feel it was like a real breakthrough when you got into this format?

NS: A total liberation!

SL: So you don't see the two Artaud series as continuous?

NS: No. They're only related in that I used Artaud's voice in both, but quite differently in each case.

SL: How is that?

NS: Because with the *Codex* it becomes more expansive in this unstructured/structured larger format. I am speaking of space and time but there are other elements, there's an added complexity in the *Codex* that's not in the paintings. This is not to disavow the paintings. They're a different kind of entity. There's a greater layering of new elements in the *Codex* that is not apparent in the earlier work—the linear extensions change impact and import.

SL: So something cosmic takes over from the subjective?

NS: Time, space, externalized.

SL: Because you do resent the purely subjective in Artaud, as in other things, right?

NS: No. His subjectivity takes on a wider scope.

MR: So how long did this series go on? From '71 to—

NS: The *Codex* was the work of two years, '71 and '72. Then I stopped. I just stopped. Suddenly it was finished. I got restless, I wanted to expand range. I didn't want to fall into a hermetic world of Artaud and myself. And I wanted to enter the repressed and violent world of subjected women. This was in line with both my career and personality becoming more externalized and working with other women, actively making decisions and activist actions. It was political in that I was talking about myself as an artist, or artist in society, even as I was again impatient to break off the old and renew my art.

MR: Did you feel, maybe, that the kind of Artaud anger was an internalized anger and you were moving towards a more active phase in your life as an artist? That's what it sounds like.

NS: Exactly. The *War Series* was externalized, intended as a public kind of manifesto, but it hit on a ferocious subjectivity. After Artaud, I deliberately moved my art away from this internalized state of victimization. In *Torture of Women*, I investigated the status of women as victims, in conditions of hell, as political prisoners in South America, Central America, Turkey. External factors were causal. Artaud's problems were due to external factors to a certain extent, but it was his mind-set, and his bodily and mental pain that informed his language.

SL: You were never tempted to go back to Artaud from a different point of view, not from need?

NS: No, the only thing I've been tempted to go back to, although I will not, is the *War Series*. I am overwhelmed by the enormity of the hatreds and purposeless violence of our political worlds, but I must pursue other directions in my art.

JUNE 10, 1995

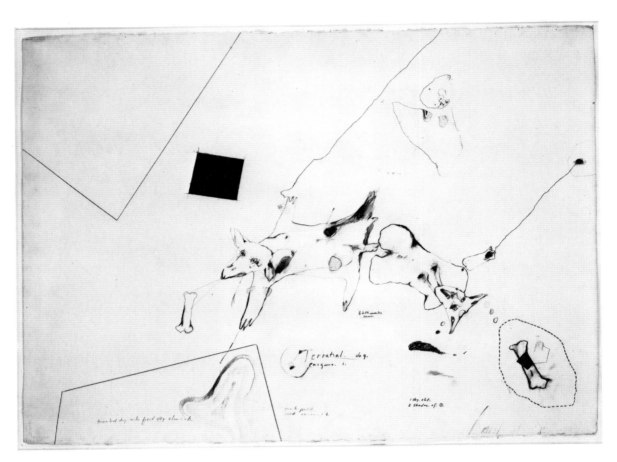

Patti Smith
Terratial Dog
1977
Crayon and colored pencil on paper
22½ x 29¾" (57.1 x 75.5 cm)
Courtesy Robert Miller Gallery

A Conversation with Patti Smith

Margit Rowell

Born in 1946, Patti Smith grew up in southern New Jersey and moved to New York in the late 1960s. A performer and celebrated rock singer since the mid-1970s, she has also published several volumes of poetry and exhibited her drawings at the Robert Miller Gallery, New York, in 1978 (alongside photographs by Robert Mapplethorpe). Her poetry and music reflect musicians of the 1960s like Bob Dylan, Jimi Hendrix, Jim Morrison, and the Rolling Stones, and such writers as William Blake, Charles Baudelaire, Arthur Rimbaud, and William Burroughs. She discovered Antonin Artaud in her late teens, first through his drawings and later taking an interest in the writings and all aspects of the man himself. As Smith talked with Margit Rowell, they looked at reproductions of Artaud's works on paper in the monograph on the drawings and portraits prepared by Paule Thévenin and published in 1986.

PATTI SMITH: My knowledge of art was really limited to my school library. My father took me to the Philadelphia Museum of Art and I was enraptured by what I saw, but I still didn't find things that I related to. At school, there weren't a lot of art books, but I did discover Dubuffet, and then I sought him out. When I got the Artaud anthology,* when I was about eighteen, and saw the couple of drawings there, I thought, This is what I was trying to say. I felt akin to the fragmentation in them. They weren't fragmented to the point of complete disorder; they were fragmented in an intelligent way, so one felt that if a person willed it, they could piece them back together. They seemed to be done with design, and a piece that he wrote, "The Human Face" [see pp. 94–97], really solidified it for me. In it he refers to "materials of human beings or animals," and you'll see in my drawings a lot of strange little animals and things.

MARGIT ROWELL: You said to me the first time we met that at first you looked at the pictures in the City Lights anthology, and that you read it later.

PS: I bought the book for the drawings.

MR: How much later did you read it and decide that this was going to be one of your manifestos?

PS: Probably within a month. I remember being so taken, first of all, with his drawings, and then with his beauty. When I was young, I thought he was a fantasy object when he was in the Carl Dreyer period. A lot of the writing, truthfully, I didn't comprehend, but I liked reading it anyway, and I remember reading that poem and thinking, That's it. There it is. I had finished high school, and that summer I

got a job in Philadelphia. I found his book in a little bookstore near the bus depot and the first thing I was attracted to was his face, so I bought his book, exactly like I bought [Rimbaud's] *Illuminations*, by falling in love with the face of the writer. Then I opened it up and saw the drawings. I was just totally taken, and I felt really happy, I felt like there was something out there, another world that I hadn't penetrated. Eventually, I was able to branch out and learn a lot more. For example, the idea of self-portraiture was very influential to me. I was also quite aware, even as a child, that we have various skins. We have our social skin, which we're constantly badgered to develop, and I remember asking my mother about this and making her very uncomfortable. As a child, I kept saying, Why do we have to react in this manner? Why, when I meet certain relatives or people that I don't like, do I have to be pleasant to them? Why do people go by a window and not break it? Why? I was amazed as a child at the discipline, I was constantly amazed that they had organized it all before I was born. I felt sort of resentful about that. I'd come onto this planet and they had it all figured out, how you're supposed to look and dress and present yourself to people. Yet here was an extremely beautiful man who was able to present himself in these other ways. It was as if he was presenting the tortured layers underneath his skin, until, at a very young age, he transfigured himself from being so beautiful to becoming like his drawings.

There is another thing, which sounds kind of funny. When I was young, I was very taken with the Declaration of Independence. We went to see that in Philadelphia when I was a little girl, and we bought a parchment scroll, a copy of it. It wasn't the words of the Declaration of Independence that struck me, it was the handwriting. I used to like to copy it, and I felt that one forgot that there was language, just looking at the writing; it was like an art form in itself. Looking just a little bit at Artaud's drawings, I felt that the writing on them was an integral part. I started combing galleries, and one man in a small gallery took a liking to me because I was always asking, Could you see these drawings for real? He had a book that was in French, with a couple of other drawings. All I remember about these drawings is the writing, the handwriting. I also went to France, in 1969 when I was about twenty-two years old, I think, or twenty-three, and I was able to see a few more Artaud drawings.

MR: Artaud, in a sense, was very angry; were you ever angry in

---

* Jack Hirschman, ed., *Antonin Artaud: An Anthology* (San Francisco: City Lights, 1965).

those years?

PS: Yes, but when I look at these drawings done at Rodez, what I always see is intelligence. I was extremely angry when I did certain drawings. But when I look at them now, I no longer see the anger. I see what I was doing graphically. Because no matter how angry one is, your intelligence is in tow. Artaud still had presence of mind, he was very conscious of his design—like Pollock's sketchbooks were very conscious, no matter how disturbed he was, or angry; the intelligence seems to take over.

MR: So would you say that the fragmentation that you see in some of your works does in fact have something to do with Artaud's Rodez drawings?

PS: Definitely.

MR: And the very stylized portraits and self-portraits also?

PS: Definitely; that was actually a conscious thing: the idea of self-portraits or portraiture as a drawing of one's inner self and not trying to do just a flattering sketch of oneself.

MR: When you later became a performer, was the example of Artaud important to you?

PS: Yes. All through my writing, all through my life, in fact, I used him as an example. Robert [Mapplethorpe] and I had some friendly arguments because he felt that I was gifted in the graphic arts and he wanted me to continue, and at that time I was introducing more and more writing in my drawing; I got to the point where I obliterated drawing and started to do drawings that had nothing but writing in them. And then I abandoned drawing totally.

MR: What year was that?

PS: 1971 or '72.

MR: After you came back from Europe the third time?

PS: Yes. I saw a big Cy Twombly show for the first time, I saw work by various artists, and I really didn't think that I had anything more to offer. My frame of mind was much better then and I felt that I knew how to do these drawings; it was becoming slick. Initially, I had done a lot of them semi-unconsciously, but as soon as I saw that I knew how to do these drawings that had been a struggle for some years, when I realized that if I wrote on them here and there they'd look really good, I lost interest in it. Robert was worried that I was spreading myself too thin. He said, You're performing, you're writing poetry, you're doing drawings—what are you going to be really good at? I used the example of Artaud; I said, It might be that I'm one of these people who're not going to be great at any one thing. I feel that Artaud's greatness was the whole package, the whole picture, the fact that he could move in these different forms of expression.

MR: Were you aware of the Living Theater in the sixties?

PS: Yes.

MR: And were there other people around you who were into Artaud?

PS: I think that there were—not like I was. I talked a lot with Sam Shepard, who was really interested in him. I branched out briefly in theater and pulled back. But as far as other artists, or writers, I never found anyone as akin to him as

myself; I think that performing artists found more kinship with him than writers. I did because of the way he moved from one form of expression to another, without being a Leonardo da Vinci; I mean, it was a different type of movement, a darker, raw-edged movement. Also, I felt he was very brave. He didn't seem at all apologetic about moving from one kind of expression to another and being slightly crude. I had that as a little badge for myself, his unapologetic way. He didn't seem to care about making his work perfect or crystallized or slick. I believe he could have.

A lot of people will say, Well you're lazy. They've said it to me: You don't want to take the time. But I've always felt, What would it prove if I went and learned all about the history of poetry and became more facile in my draftsmanship? One of the things I've always tried to do in performing is keep pushing to discover things. I can't do it with the same energy as when I was younger because it nearly killed me. I got to the point where I thought I was going to perhaps get electrocuted on stage doing things sonically with guitar and feedback. Or I pushed myself to tell a story or find some emotional or mental place where I was skewing language, or chanting, or doing something that no one had ever done, and also forcing all of us—myself, my band, the audience—to reveal other layers of existence. People would write about my performances as being painful, and sometimes they were; sometimes they were joyous and sometimes painful. I've had whole performances where nothing seemed to go right. I'd get extremely angry, and no language would come out. That's why I started playing electric guitar. I never learned chords, I didn't learn notes, I dealt with sound. I was really interested to see how you could push it further and get past the skeleton, into the entrails of the instrument.

This is another reason why I didn't go into theater, because when you take the philosophy of somebody like Artaud, and then build a theater or ideas around it, you're approximating what he was doing. But he actually felt the things, so I always thought that theatrical presentations based on his work were too dogmatic. But what are you going to do? Are you going to kill somebody on stage? You have to have some kind of restraint, and I contemplated that for a while, because I never wanted to hurt anybody. So what do you do? I felt that instead of dealing with it as a physical experience, you have to try to open up the brain, layer after layer, finding all the levels of experience or anguish. Didn't he write that he had a claw in the brain? I remember writing that down. I used to feel that I knew exactly what he was talking about.

MR: Can I ask you if you ever took drugs?

PS: At the time I was brought up, in the early sixties, I only knew about drugs through art; I knew that jazz musicians took drugs, and I read Théophile Gautier, and that's how I learned about drugs. I was completely fascinated with drugs, but as a tool for artists. I had a snobbish attitude: I was horrified at the idea of the common man taking drugs. I really felt that you had to be initiated. I tried a drug here and there in the early seventies, but I always had to work after I took drugs. If I tried cocaine, I'd write a poem about it. I felt it was important to either draw or write while I was taking a drug because I felt honor-bound. I didn't get deeply involved in anything until I really started smoking pot quite a bit in 1977 til '79, but even then, I wrote all the time. I've never been a social drug taker. People have written all kinds of things about me and drugs, and it's fantasy, really.

MR: Do you feel that what you did under the influence of drugs was better than what you did without it?

PS: Well, when I was younger, I thought so. As much abandon as some artists have in their work, they are austere as well. I have a disciplined side to my personality, extremely austere, reserved, and self-protective, and I think that I often felt that I wouldn't be able to do work because that aspect of me would take over. I'd go sometimes several days without drawing or writing or expressing myself; I'd feel almost like an alcoholic who doesn't have a drink—unfulfilled, depressed. If I was smoking pot I could write all the time, so I started feeling that it was important to my work, especially my writing. I gave up all drugs in 1980 when I got married and then had children. So I had to start all over again. I had to start learning to write and draw not only without being stoned, which was a little difficult at first, but then having no atmosphere. You know, the *atmosphere*: it's three in the morning, I'm stoned, I'm staying up all night, and I'm going to draw. I couldn't have that anymore. I had children, I had to start living a totally different life—

MR: But that was a choice.

PS: Yes. If I wanted to do any drawings or writing, I had to get up at five in the morning, before my baby got up, and sit and do it. I learned, and it was a hard lesson, that I actually did just as well, if not necessarily better. It was very painful, because I had to let go of a lot of my ideas about muses, drugs, and certain mystical things, and I had to face the fact that it was actually myself who was doing this work. I wasn't necessarily a mouthpiece of the gods. It's very hard for certain people to accept that they have a gift, a calling, independent of demons and things, and I think that if they can't accept that, it destroys them. I think that is the kind of man Artaud was. He just couldn't accept his own inner beauty and he did everything to deface it, disguise it, thwart it. I've been like that in my own way. He was a constant source of comfort, justification, for how I was. I used him continuously to justify my act, my performances, my way of being, and I felt, especially when I got a lot of criticism for what I was doing—I was taking things too far, I was pushing the envelope in a destructive way—I always felt I had him above me to draw from.

MR: You took your Artaud anthology with you to Mexico?

PS: I traveled light. I remember I had one William Burroughs book and my Artaud book, and I had some paper. I got really ill in Mexico, I had fevers, and I did portraits of him, from the photographs of him in that book, and I taped them to the wall of the hotel room. I left there in such a poor state that I forgot to take them, and I still sometimes see them lined up, about seven portraits of him.

MR: Well, now it comes back to me why I wanted you to go and see the movie [*En compagnie d'Antonin Artaud* (*My Life and Times with Antonin Artaud*), 1993]. The sequence in which Artaud is rehearsing Colette Thomas—we know that she went crazy, that she was initially unstable, but he almost drove her off the edge—was rather extraordinary.

PS: I understood that section, almost humorously, because I knew exactly what was going on. What happens is that you get involved with people who really want to give you what you want to get because they love you so much, even though you're cruel. It's not an intentional cruelty—someone could look at that scene and think, Oh, he's such a bastard—but if you've been there in some way yourself, you know it's that you have such a vision, you get so intense and focused, that you cease to deal with the fragile human aspect of people because you just want to go from intense mind to intense mind and get the work done. It's like the work becomes more important than either yourself or the other person. Of course that scene is in a movie, but it wasn't his intent to be cruel to that girl. He wanted to draw out of her what he knew wasn't in that poor girl; it was in him.

MR: They say that the best art and the best writing is done with some kind of critical distance. But though I'm sure, as you were saying about the drawings, that he had some critical distance, critical intelligence, he also wanted to show raw feeling from the inside. How do you coordinate these two things?

PS: You have to be the master of your game. I think his falling was—and I shouldn't comment on it because I don't know enough about it—getting so intensely involved in drugs.

MR: He couldn't do without them. He was in pain.

PS: What happens, though—having seen it with people that I know—you don't do drugs for free. Drugs do intensify certain areas of your brain or psyche, but others are deteriorating, and one loses balance. And I think that when one loses balance, no matter how brilliant one is, you're going to lose a hold on it. I think he was so brilliant that even at his worst, he could still hold the reins. But people do let go of the reins, and then you have chaos, you cease to have art.

MR: But you don't think that there was chaos in his drawings, like the ones that we looked at?

PS: I don't think he lived long enough for that. I think perhaps had he kept living, one might have started seeing total disintegration, although you would also see glimpses of brilliance. But no matter what these drawings look like, he was quite aware of what he was doing. Some people wouldn't agree with that, but having explored areas of that place myself, I'd say he was quite aware. You just can't present a sheet of paper like that unless you're pretty aware of what you're doing.

AUGUST 9, 1995

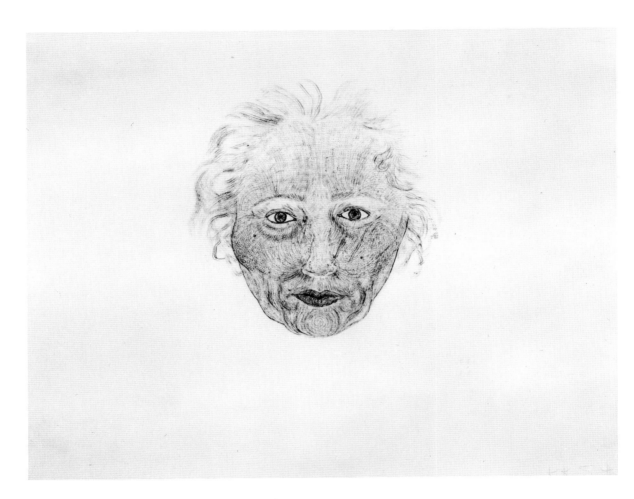

Kiki Smith
Goodwitch
1993
Ink
19 x 26" (48.3 x 66 cm)
Courtesy PaceWildenstein

A Conversation with Kiki Smith

Sylvère Lotringer

Kiki Smith, born in Nuremberg, Germany, in 1954, has lived and worked as an artist in New York City since the mid-1970s. Since 1980 she has created installations and sculpture in mediums ranging from paper to cast glass and bronze, as well as drawings and prints, in which elements of the human body become a vehicle for a wide-ranging exploration of the body's significance. As Smith talked with Sylvère Lotringer, they looked at reproductions of Artaud's works on paper in the monograph on the drawings and portraits by Paule Thévenin.

SYLVÈRE LOTRINGER: How long have you known about Artaud?

KIKI SMITH: I basically know nothing about Artaud except from Nancy Spero's Artaud drawings. Nancy Spero is somebody whose work is very significant to me, particularly the *Codex Artaud* drawings—the combination of the texts and the visual, how they go together. After seeing her drawings, I saw the Thévenin monograph of Artaud's drawings, in 1986. I used to draw pictures and then for about ten years stopped drawing. I didn't feel confident about the way that I draw because I didn't learn how and I draw in a very stylized way. But with certain things in my life changing, in about 1990, I started making drawings again actively, and I started drawing pictures of faces.

SL: Which faces?

KS: Of mine, pretty much mine. Nobody would ever recognize them as me particularly; nobody has ever thought they look like drawings of me.

SL: Was that deliberate?

KS: No, it's because I can't do any better. I couldn't pay attention to details until about 1990. I wasn't calm enough. The way I like drawing is just to look at all the details and try to draw them, and before, I was just too anxious. Drawing is something where you have a really direct, immediate relationship with the material, with the paper and pencil in front of you. So you make a mark, and then you make another mark in relation to that mark, whereas with a lot of my sculpture, I have a concept, and then it's labor. With drawing, you're in the present; it's more like painting; you are making decisions. I couldn't really handle the anxiety of that until a couple of years ago, and then I enjoyed it as a secret nighttime activity, to look into a little mirror and make the drawings. So after doing that, I thought about the Artaud drawings again and how wonderful the energy in them is. Maybe it's how the lines are put on the pages and how they're smudged, or how

there's a concentration of line. Mine are sort of super-all-over exactly the same, but these Artaud drawings have tremendous energy and physicality. In drawing you take physical energy out of your body and put it directly onto a page. In these drawings that intensity is really evident.

SL: Do you try to make drawings that are faithful to what you see in the mirror?

KS: I try. They just don't turn out that way. They all look alike, but they don't really look like me. I like funerary masks. When you see funerary masks in museums, they are flattened out, and they have this stretching of the face like the Egyptian goddess Hathor. A lot of those faces are extended and made flat, like topographical maps.

SL: That's what happened in some of the self-portraits you made.

KS: They get unfolded. I like unfolding bodies, flattening them out and looking at them. So I'm always distorting a little bit, trying to pull it around, separating the form from the matter.

SL: That's part of it not being recognizable.

KS: Maybe. Artaud's drawings are really great because the skin of the people also has all these lesions. People get a lot of sores.

SL: It's like the body's porous; there is a point where it is very difficult to tell the inside from the outside.

KS: Well that is because the distinction doesn't exist. Physically, you are as porous as outer space; you are a totally porous, open structure.

SL: Right. Artaud may offer a privileged example of the passage from a kind of generality of the body to something very specific, which he calls "the body without organs." I wonder how you came to make the drawings?

KS: I started by thinking about the skin as a system of the body. What I like about the skin is the surface detail, and that it can be unfolded; you can look at it as an envelope or something.

SL: A body bag.

KS: And so for me, drawing has been more about trying to look at details. I'd been interested in hirsutism. For a while I was making drawings of women with facial hair. What I like is obsessive detail, trying to draw all the hairs on the head. And I like that in other people's drawings, because it's really over the top. It's a kind of meditation or freedom to just get obsessed by trying to draw everything. It's also about getting older. When I was younger there was less detail, and all of a sudden I'm beginning to get wrinkles, you can see the future smacking you in the head. But being in my forties now, it's much more interesting to draw myself than it was when I was twenty-five because there was much less of me present.

SL: The lines of experience—the face becomes more individualized, while the body can be much more generic.

KS: Well, I like that you can subtly manipulate faces, bring focus to features, unfold them. I like the immediacy, the attentiveness: it's sort of meditative and relaxing.

SL: So first it was something that made you nervous, and then it became something relaxing?

KS: That happens with a lot of work. Part of it is that you have too much attachment to the results, how it turns out, rather than wanting the experience of it. Sometimes I get anxious before doing a piece. It takes me months or years to do certain things because I know there's such a deep connection to my identity, so I avoid them for a long time. But then once you start working, you just forget your fear and try to be in the present. That's one great thing about art: you get to be in the present when you're making.

SL: In a self-portrait, you're really confronted with yourself but at the same time you take yourself as an object.

KS: You get free of yourself, which is kind of what one strives for in life. Now I'm making some portraits with moles all over the faces; they're like constellations. You don't have to make them look right. I think that the mutilation is really a big pleasure in making representations, that you can manipulate and mutilate the surface, make it more grotesque; I think there's a lot of freedom.

SL: Mutilation is a heavy word—

KS: Or distorting. Or whatever. But I think that for women in particular, who are being defined by looks, that to fuck up their looks is one strategy that people take in their real lives to avoid the confinement of being defined through the physical in a way that's narrow. Culturally, in the United States, you have extremely narrow possibilities for the physical manifestation of women. Women exist in an extremely wide variety of appearances, but they are always having to measure themselves in terms of very confining images, and so I think mutilation is powerful. It might turn on you and be annihilating in some ways, too, but I think it is something that people are very attracted to. There is all this stuff about young women cutting themselves. In one way, it's like a proof of existence, and in another, it's a proof of healing—I mean, you're mutilated and you survive. Certainly in the Artaud drawings there's a lot of mutilation. And I think that there's pleasure in that, especially when it's imaging of the self. But whether it's the self or not, I think that people want to cut vent holes, make holes in the body, to let themselves out, to get out of the confines of the self.

SL: Obviously Artaud wasn't responding to the situation of being a woman. He was hardly a man to start with.

KS: When you can't figure it out in ways other than the physical, you make a manifestation of reality, a physical metaphor for reality, and you want to puncture its surface to get out, to get free from it, from whatever definitions are too confining. So some people play it out on themselves physically, and maybe in this country people do it because we don't have a political practice that teaches us to play it out in the streets, so people turn it on themselves more. Maybe it's improper and misdirected and isn't necessarily a successful strategy for your life, but it certainly is a concrete option. I think there's a lot of pleasure in it, and making drawings is a very safe way to play it out. I mean, you're not sticking holes in yourself, though maybe you're doing that too.

SL: Artaud was burning holes in paper, too. There was an exorcistic aspect to it. And that was also some sort of a body metaphor.

KS: To alleviate pressure; either internal pressure or external pressure. You already have all these orifices and you also have your skin as a big orifice, but people get used to those, and so they need some more.

SL: Some people want fewer. In *Naked Lunch*, Burroughs wondered why we have a nose and ears and mouth and an asshole; shouldn't we have like one big black hole?

KS: I like a variety. For a couple of years, a lot of my work was just basically about orifices, and different body fluids and language and foreign substances that go in and out through orifices. And the skin is an orifice; certainly pus and things like that come out of the skin. It's also like the inside world making itself evident, becoming physical. Which is also a very Catholic version of life, for the body to physically manifest nonphysical or metaphysical or spiritual concerns; to make stigmata, to make evidence. I think that's why Christ works as a metaphor: the suffering is made flesh.

SL: It's like a sacrificial element.

KS: Well, manifesting suffering in the flesh is something that European artists have used as a big model for representational work.

SL: Are you yourself aware of that element in your work, of a relation to Catholicism?

KS: At different times I have different interests. I have been interested in the Catholic representation of the body. A lot of Catholicism is really detrimental in one's daily life, and ultimately my concern is my survival in my daily life. Sometimes it's interesting to see how you're owned by the Christian or Judeo-Christian history of Europe, and how and where it shows up in positive or negative aspects of your life. I used to think about hierarchical dualism as sort of a base of European thinking and how destructive it is. I think less about it now—

SL: Artaud is steeped in that Christian tradition. He fought it but he was totally imbued with it.

KS: Yes, but those are the ones who fight it. People who aren't owned by it don't bother. I am definitely owned by it— maybe less now than I used to be—

SL: So you think your concern with the body has something to do with it as well?

KS: Not necessarily. The body seems like a good place to talk about being here. And certainly, as a place, it is informed by how it has been represented.

SL: It's been codified.

KS: That is how you understand it, through languages. The Italians have a really different version of suffering than the Germans, or the Spanish—the Mexican-Spanish tradition. The Northern version of suffering changes at different times in history. But definitely that physicality of suffering, like Christ sweating blood and all the holes in the body, or in the Middle Ages, with all those people eating spider webs all day or starving themselves. It changes. Certainly in my short lifetime the body has changed radically as a space.

SL: Why do you think people work on their bodies so much—I mean asceticism, suffering, emaciation—

KS: Well, it's how we're here. I mean, it's the physical form in which we're here and it is the only thing that we share with other people. It's the form, it's where our consciousness chooses to be.

SL: And how does this form relate to the formal aspects that you were talking about in Artaud's drawings?

KS: I mean that you understand and read drawings through the concentration of marks and the evidence of energy. Materials have different physical, formal qualities that you read according to their social histories as well as physiologically, how you interact with them. You recognize when somebody knows how to manifest energy in a physically contained space. If you look at Artaud's drawings, you recognize that he knows something. I don't really know what to do with what he knows; I can't say, Oh, yeah, he's smudging. It's not the smudging, because everybody knows smudging. Everybody can see that you smudge a little here, or you have loose lines and precise lines. It's just somehow how he puts it together in a way that gives you information you didn't have before.

SL: Artaud's drawings didn't hit you right away. The impact came after—

KS: The way Nancy Spero drew, the way she combined the aggressive language of Artaud with the aggressiveness of the physicality of her drawings made me want to look at his drawings. That kind of erasing and annihilating images. The self-mutilation, too, the anger and hatred, either self-hatred or hatred of other people. It's both aggressive and pleasurable.

SL: That's true for the language as well.

KS: There is something really interesting about seeing text and drawing together; language and drawing together cast very special kinds of spells. Something magical definitely happens, something that is manipulative—and difficult, because there's something very seductive about it, but then the words have meaning. It's always in a way more pleasurable when you don't have to understand what they say. It's a sort of physical possession or magic happening. The way you read it is a kind of intoxicating hocus-pocus. Even when it's just his name and the date—all of that is part of his portraits where it's all floating around his head. With most artists, the combination of language and pictures is different than just pictures or just language.

But in a heavy way, in a profound way; it's doing something physiological to you.

SL: What's the most expressive thing? What has most power in the face? Is it the eyes? Or doesn't it matter?

KS: When they trace people's vision, people go eyes-mouth, eyes-mouth; they make a triangle: eyes-mouth. So probably that's what people look at or are attracted to. I like the wrinkles and the moles and spots and little scars. But I also am very aware of these things and fascinated by them on other people's bodies. To me—I realize in a sort of nutty way—I find I like people with scars and things because they're like holes to me. Besides being holes where they can get out, they're holes where you can get in, possible entrances into somebody's body. These are defects that other people maybe don't like in themselves but it makes them vulnerable. Maybe you make drawings and then hack the people to bits so you can make them vulnerable. Christ with holes in him, or Osiris, are our models; these ripped-up human bodies, they are our gods, and they're our entries to the sacred. Certainly in Christianity, unlike Buddhism, our attachment to suffering is our model for transcendence; also in Christianity you have a big thing about transcendence of the body and body-hatred. On the flip side, you have reliquaries, the preservation and worship of body fragments.

SL: There's something about the body that's both attractive and repulsive. And anything that involves attraction/repulsion belongs to the realm of the sacred.

KS: But, like with Osiris, it is really deep in the model.

SL: It's all in pieces anyway.

KS: Yeah, he's all totally shredded apart. And then bound back together; kind of bandaged up or mended. And this is the vehicle, this mutilated body, or Christ with holes in him, or people all around the world getting stigmata and making physical manifestations of the impermanence and also of the possibility of entry.

SL: The imperfection is also the most perfect because it is like the stigmata. I mean, the sacred wound. It marks a presence.

KS: But the wound in itself is the presence of God; our model of God is a wound. God and Jesus and Osiris are things that defy the wound, too; they're both killed and resurrected. They're springtime gods. And then there's Doctor Frankenstein's creature.

SL: Do you internalize this at all? I mean Christ and all this—

KS: I think people are the internalization of history models. I think that what we're trying to do, being in a certain time period, is to figure out what belief systems we're attached to, and trying to have—you can't really have clarity, but—have some distance from how you're owned by it all. But I also like to think about all that stuff; to me, spiritual life and different cosmologies, mappings of spiritual life, are the most interesting things.

SL: Is the body also a spiritual point of entry?

KS: Well, the body does represent a spiritual journey. That's what you're doing here. I guess I'm a hocus-pocus believer.

JUNE 16, 1995

Catalogue of the Exhibition

This catalogue documents the objects shown in the exhibition *Antonin Artaud: Works on Paper* at The Museum of Modern Art, New York, October 1, 1996–January 7, 1997. Generally the titles are those assigned by Paule Thévenin in Thévenin and Jacques Derrida, *Antonin Artaud: Dessins et portraits* (Paris: Gallimard; Munich: Schirmer-Mosel Verlag, 1986). Works included in that catalogue are identified in the following entries by the abbreviation P.T.-J.D., followed by the reference number assigned in the book. In many cases, Thévenin determined titles from lists made by Artaud in his notebooks. The titles of the "spells" derive from the names of those to whom Artaud addressed them, indicated in the letter or on the envelope, and those of the portraits from the names of the individuals depicted. Titles of drawings made at Rodez have usually been provided by an inscription on the drawing.

Dates that include day and month are based on the artist's inscriptions. Approximate dates were determined by secondary sources, including Artaud's lists in the notebooks and recollections of the sitters for his portraits. In transcribed inscriptions, a solidus marks a line break, and the term "glossolalia" indicates passages of words invented by Artaud. Full titles of exhibitions referred to below by year and place are given in the Exhibition History (p. 163).

1
Self-Portrait
c. 1915
Charcoal
5⅞ x 4" (15 x 10 cm)
Not signed, not dated
P.T.-J.D. 10
Provenance: Marie-Ange Malausséna
Exhibited: 1995, Marseille, no. 2, ill. p. 71
Private collection

2
Spell for Lise Deharme
5 September 1937
India ink on burned and soiled paper
10½ x 8¼" (27 x 21 cm)
Signed and dated (in cabalistic figures); inscribed: "Je ferai enfoncer / une croix de fer / rougie au feu dans ton / sexe puant de Juive / et cabotinerai ensuite / sur ton cadavre pour / te prouver qu'il y a / ENCORE DES DIEUX!" ["I will have a red-hot iron cross rammed into your stinking Jewess's hole and then I'll trample all over your dead body to prove to you that GODS STILL EXIST!"]
P.T.-J.D. 36
Provenance: André Breton
Exhibited: 1987, Paris, no. 8; 1995,

Marseille, no. 14, ill. p. 88
Fonds André Breton, Bibliothèque Littéraire Jacques Doucet, Paris

3
Spell for Jacqueline Breton
17 September 1937
India ink
9¾ x 7⅞" (25 x 20 cm)
Not signed, dated (in cabalistic figures); inscribed: "J'envoie un Sort / au Premier qui osera / vous toucher. / Je lui mettrai, en bouillie sa petite gueule de faux coq / orgueilleux. / Je le fesserai devant / 100 000 personnes! / SA PEINTURE QUI N'A / JAMAIS RIEN EU DE TRÈS / ÉCLATANT EST DEVENUE / DEFINITIVEMENT / MAUVAISE / IL A UNE TROP LAIDE / VOIX / C'EST L'ANTÉCHRIST" ["I'm sending a Spell to the First One who will dare touch you. I'll crush his braggart's little snooty snout to pulp. I'll spank him in front of 100,000 people! HIS PAINTINGS WHICH NEVER WERE THAT GREAT HAVE DEFINITELY BECOME LOUSY. HE'S GOT TOO UGLY A VOICE. HE'S THE ANTICHRIST"]
P.T.-J.D. 37
Provenance: Jacqueline Breton; André Breton
Exhibited: 1987, Paris, no. 9; 1995, Marseille, no. 15, ill. p. 89
Fonds André Breton, Bibliothèque Littéraire Jacques Doucet, Paris

4
Spell for Léon Fouks
8 May 1939
Wax crayon on burned paper
8¼ x 5¼" (21 x 13.5 cm)
Executed on the third page of a
signed and dated letter; inscribed:
"Gardez ce Sort sur votre coeur. Et en
cas de / danger touchez votre coeur
avec / l'Index et le Medius de la Main
/ Droite ET LE SORT S'ECLAIRERA."
["Keep this Spell against your heart.
And in case of danger touch your
heart with the Index and Middle
Fingers of your Right Hand AND
THE SPELL WILL ILLUMINATE."]
P.T.-J.D. 38
Exhibited: 1987, Paris, no. 10, ill.
p. 19; 1995, Marseille, no. 16, ill. p. 91
Private collection

5 (recto-verso).
Spell for Sonia Mossé
14 May 1939
Wax crayon on burned paper
8¼ x 5¼" (21 x 13.5 cm)
Executed on the third and fourth
pages of a signed and dated letter;
inscribed (recto): "Tu vivras morte /
tu n'arrêteras plus / de trépasser et
de descendre / Je te lance / une Force
de Mort"; (verso): "Et ce Sort / ne
sera pas rapporté. / Il ne s[era] pas /
reporté. / Et il brise / tout envoûte-
ment. Et ce sort / ag[i]t immédiate-
ment." [(recto): "You will live as
dead, you will never stop the process
of dying and descending. I cast upon
you a Force of Death" (verso): "And
this Spell will not be recalled. It will
not be deferred. And it breaks all

other witch's spells. And this spell
will act instantly."]
P.T.-J.D. 39 recto-verso
Exhibited: 1995, Marseille, no. 17,
ill. pp. 92–93
Bibliothèque Nationale de France

6 (recto-verso)
Spell for Roger Blin
c. 22 May 1939
Ink, wax crayon, and gouache on
burned paper
8¼ x 5¼" (21 x 13.5 cm)
Signed verso, not dated; inscribed
(recto): "Tous ceux qui / se sont
concertés po[ur] / m'empêcher /
de prendre d[e] / L'HÉROÏNE /
tous ceu[x] qui ont / [to]uché à Anne
Man- / son à cause de cela / le
dimanche / [21] Mai 1939, je les /
[fer]ai [per]ce[r] vivant[s]"; (verso):
"sur une place [de] / PARIS e[t] je
leur / ferai perforer et / brûle[r] les
moëlles. / [Je] suis dans un Asile /
d'Aliénés mais ce / rêve d'un Fou
sera / réalisé et il se[ra] / réalisé par
Moi. / Antonin Artaud" [(recto): "All
those who banded together to prevent
me from taking HEROIN, all those
who touched Anne Manson because
of that Sunday 21 May 1939, I'll
have them pierced alive"; (verso):
"in a PARIS square and I'll have
their marrows perforated and burned.
I am in an Insane Asylum but this
dream of a Madman will become true
and will be implemented by Me.
Antonin Artaud."]
P.T.-J.D. 41 recto-verso
Provenance: Roger Blin;
Paule Thévenin
Exhibited: 1987, Paris, no. 11; 1995,
Marseille, no. 18, ill. pp. 94-95
Bibliothèque Nationale de France.
Bequest of Paule Thévenin, 1994

7 (recto-verso)
Spell for Hitler
c. September 1939
Wax crayon on burned paper
8¼ x 5¼" (21 x 13.5 cm)
Signed, not dated; inscribed (recto):
"Ville-Evrard / HITLER / Chancelier
du Reich / Cher Monsieur / Je vous
avais montré en 1932 / au Café de . . .
à Berlin l'un / des soirs où nous avons
fait connais- / sance et peu avant que
vous / ne preniez le pouvoir, les
barrages / que j'avais établis sur une
/ carte qui n'était pas qu'une / carte
de géographie contre / une acte de
force dirigée / dans un certain
nombre de / sens que vous me
désigniez. / Je lève aujourd'hui Hitler
/ les barrages que j'avais mis! / Les
Parisiens ont besoin / de gaz / Je suis
votre / Antonin Artaud." (verso):
"P.S. Bien entendu cher Monsieur
ceci est à peine une invita- / tion:
c'est surtout un / avertissement. / S'il
vous plaît, comme à / tout Initié de
ne pas en tenir / compte ou de faire
semblant de / ne pas en tenir compte
à votre / aise. Je me garde. / Gardez-
vous! / La purulence des Initiés
Français a atteint au paroxysme du
spasme / d'ailleurs vous le saviez."
[(recto): "Ville-Evrard. HITLER.
Chancellor of the Reich. Dear Sir: On
one of those evenings we met in 1932,
at the Café . . . in Berlin, shortly
before you came to power, I showed
you the barriers that I had set up on a
map that was not just geographical,
designed to block an act of force
directed in a number of directions,
such as you had indicated to me.
Today, Hitler, I am eliminating these
barriers! The Parisians need gas. I
remain your Antonin Artaud."
(verso): "P.S. Obviously dear Sir this
is hardly an invitation: it is above all
a warning. If you choose, as all
Initiates do, not to pay attention to
it or to pretend not to, suit yourself.
I protect myself. Watch out! The

purulence of French Initiates has
reached a paroxysm of spasm,
moreover you knew that."]
P.T.-J.D. 42
Exhibited: 1987, Paris, no. 12; 1995,
Marseille, no. 19, ill. p. 96
Private collection

8
Untitled
c. February 1944
Charcoal
10½ x 7⅛" (27 x 18 cm)
Not signed, not dated
P.T.-J.D. 43
Provenance: Alain Cuny
Exhibited: 1987, Paris, no. 13; 1995,
Marseille, no. 20, ill. p. 97
Private collection

9
Untitled
c. February 1944
Charcoal
10¼ x 6⅝" (26.5 x 17.5 cm)
Not signed, not dated
P.T.-J.D. 44
Provenance: Paule Thévenin
Exhibited: 1987, Paris, no. 14; 1994,
Paris; 1995, Marseille, no. 21, ill. p. 98
Musée National d'Art Moderne—
Centre de Création Industrielle,
Centre Georges Pompidou, Paris.
Bequest of Paule Thévenin, 1993

10
Untitled
c. February 1944
Charcoal
10¼ x 6⅝" (26.5 x 17.5 cm)
Not signed, not dated
P.T.-J.D. 45
Provenance: Paule Thévenin
Exhibited: 1987, Paris, no. 15; 1994,
Paris; 1995, Marseille, no. 22,
ill. p. 99
Musée National d'Art Moderne—
Centre de Création Industrielle,
Centre Georges Pompidou, Paris.
Bequest of Paule Thévenin, 1993

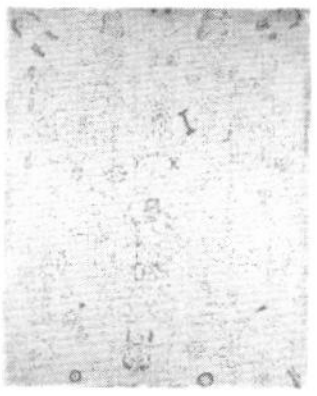

11
"L'être et ses foetus . . ."
[Being and its fetuses]
c. January 1945
Graphite and wax crayon
25¼ x 19⅝" (64 x 50 cm)
Not signed, not dated; inscribed:
"L'être et ses foetus / utérines
viscères ce crime anal des êtres /
les Chimères Gérard de Nerval /
[glossolalia] / en moi ma fille
Catherine lama" ["Being and its
fetuses uterine entrails, this anal
crime of beings, the Chimeras of
Gérard de Nerval [glossolalia] in me
my daughter Catherine *lama*"]
P.T.-J.D. 46
Provenance: Marcel Bisiaux
Exhibited: 1980, Les Sables d'Olonne,
no. 12; 1987, Paris, no. 16; 1995,
Marseille, no. 23, ill. p. 106
Private collection

12
The Hanged Woman (La Pendue)
c. January 1945
Graphite and wax crayon
25½ x 19⅝" (65 x 50 cm)
Signed lower right, not dated;
inscribed: "Catherine"
P.T.-J.D. 49
Provenance: Marcel Bisiaux
Exhibited: 1987, Paris, no. 19; 1995,
Marseille, no. 26, ill. p. 111
Private collection

13
"L'immaculée conception . . ."
[The immaculate conception]
c. January 1945
Graphite and wax crayon
24 x 18¾" (61 x 48 cm)
Not signed, not dated; inscribed:
"L'immaculée conception / fut
l'assassinat du principe / de
l'HOMME / qui est un canon monté
sur roues" ["The immaculate
conception was the assassination
of the principle of MAN who is a
cannon mounted on wheels"]
P.T.-J.D. 48
Exhibited: 1947, Paris; 1979, Paris,
no. 16, ill. p. 57; 1980, Les Sables
d'Olonne, no. 15; 1987, Paris, no. 18;
1995, Marseille, no. 25, ill. p. 109
Private collection

14
"Jamais réel et toujours vrai . . ."
[Never real and always true]
c. January 1945
Graphite and wax crayon
25¼ x 18⅞" (64 x 48 cm)
Not signed, not dated; inscribed:
"Jamais réel et toujours vrai /
non pas de l'art mais de / la ra-tée de
Soudan et de Dahomey" ["Never
real and always true, not art but the
ra-tée of Sudan and Dahomey"]
P.T.-J.D. 47
Provenance: Marcel Bisiaux
Exhibited: 1980, Les Sables d'Olonne,
no. 13; 1987, Paris, no. 17; 1995,
Marseille, no. 24, ill. p. 107
Private collection

15
Couti l'anatomie
c. September 1945
Graphite and wax crayon
25⅞ x 19⅝" (65.5 x 50 cm)
Signed lower right, not dated;
inscribed: "Anie / couti d'arbac /
arbac cata / les os sema"
P.T.-J.D. 50
Provenance: Anie Besnard-Faure
Exhibited: 1947, Paris; 1976, Paris,
ill. p. 136; 1980, Les Sables d'Olonne,
no. 9; 1987, Paris, no. 20, ill. p. 33;
1995, Marseille, no. 27, ill. p. 113;
1995, Paris, no. 5, ill. p. 74
Musée National d'Art Moderne—
Centre de Création Industrielle,
Centre Georges Pompidou, Paris

16 (recto)
"La potence du gouffre . . ."
[The gallows for the abyss]
c. October 1945
Graphite and wax crayon
24 ⅞ x 18 ⅞" (63 x 48 cm)
Not signed, not dated; inscribed:
"La potence du gouffre / est l'être et
non / son âme / et c'est son corps."
["The gallows for the abyss is the
being and not his soul and it is his
body."]
P.T.-J.D. 51 recto
Provenance: Gaston Ferdière;
Matarasso; Irène Nomikosoff
Exhibited: 1987, Paris, no. 21; 1995,
Marseille, no. 28, ill. p. 114
Musée National d'Art Moderne—
Centre de Création Industrielle,
Centre Georges Pompidou, Paris

16 (verso)
*The Soldier with a Gun
(Le Soldat au fusil)*
c. October 1945–January 1946
Graphite and wax crayon
24⅞ x 18⅞" (63 x 48 cm)
Not signed, not dated; inscribed:
"Le temps des / lâches passera /
sous la / guerre du canon." ["The
cowards' season will pass under
the cannon's fire."]
P.T.-J.D. 51 verso
Provenance: Gaston Ferdière;
Matarasso; Irène Nomikosoff
Exhibited: 1987, Paris, no. 21,
ill. p. 35; 1995, Marseille, no. 28,
ill. p. 117
Musée National d'Art Moderne—
Centre de Création Industrielle,
Centre Georges Pompidou, Paris

17
"Poupou rabou..."
c. December 1945
Graphite and wax crayon
25½ x 19⅝" (65 x 50 cm)
Signed lower center and lower right,
not dated; inscribed: "Poupou rabou /
[glossolalia]"
P.T.-J.D. 52
Provenance: Marcel Bisiaux
Exhibited: 1987, Paris, no. 22; 1995,
Marseille, no. 29, ill. p. 119
Private collection

18
The Totem (Le Totem)
c. December 1945–February 1946
Graphite and wax crayon
24⅞ x 18⅞" (63 x 48 cm)
Signed lower right, not dated
P.T.-J.D. 53
Provenance: Marthe Robert; Jacques
Prevel; Bernard Noël
Exhibited: 1947, Paris; 1976, Paris,
ill. p. 148; 1980, Les Sables d'Olonne,
no. 24; 1987, Paris, no. 23, ill. p. 29;
1995, Marseille, no. 35, ill. p. 131;
1995, Geneva, no. 2, ill. p. 77
Musée Cantini, Marseille

19
"Les illusions de l'âme"
[The illusions of the soul]
c. January 1946
Graphite and wax crayon
24⅞ x 18⅞" (63 x 48 cm)
Signed lower center, not dated;
inscribed: "Les illusions de l'âme"
["The illusions of the soul"]
P.T.-J.D. 58
Provenance: Jean Dequeker; Gaston
Ferdière; Matarasso; Irène
Nomikosoff; Michel Ellenberger
Exhibited: 1987, Paris, no. 27; 1993,
Paris, no. 1002; 1995, Marseille,
no. 32, ill. p. 127
Musée National d'Art Moderne—
Centre de Création Industrielle,
Centre Georges Pompidou, Paris.
Gift of Michel Ellenberger, 1987

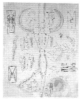

20
The Minotaur (Le Minotaure)
c. January 1946
Graphite and wax crayon
24⅞ x 18⅞" (63 x 48 cm)
Not signed, not dated
P.T.-J.D. 56
Provenance: Marcel Bisiaux
Exhibited: 1966, Bern, ill.; 1980,
Les Sables d'Olonne, no. 14; 1987,
Paris, no. 25; 1995, Marseille, no. 33,
ill. p. 40
Private collection

21 (recto)
Untitled
c. January 1946
Graphite
25 ½ x 19 ⅝" (65 x 50 cm)
Not signed, not dated
P.T.-J.D. 57 recto
Provenance: Luis Cardoza y Aragon,
Mexico
Exhibited: 1987, Paris, no. 26, ill.
p. 31; 1995, Marseille, no. 31, ill p. 123
Musée National d'Art Moderne—
Centre de Création Industrielle,
Centre Georges Pompidou, Paris

21 (verso)
The Machine of Being
(*La Machine de l'être*) or
"Dessin à regarder de traviole..."
[Drawing to be looked at askew]
c. January 1946
Graphite and wax crayon
25 ½ x 19 ⅝" (65 x 50 cm)
Signed lower right, not dated;
inscribed: "dessin à regarder de
traviole / au bas d'un mur en se /
frottant le dessous / du bras droit
Yvonne ira mais / ça n'ira / pas
encore une boîte dans Ra / Sedi man
/ d'Anta Mede / et mede qui sera /
après le souffle roule / dans la rotule
la conscience / te vomira / Après le
kaduka, l'os de la poussière / moudre
des tibias / cenac / diktbur / varzur /
kandash" ["drawing to be looked at
askew at the base of a wall while
rubbing the underside of the right
arm. Yvonne will be alright but it
will not yet be alright a box in *Ra*

Sedi man d'Anta Mede and *mede* will
be after your breath reaches your
knee-cap your conscience will vomit
you out. After the *Kaduka*, the dust's
bone grinds the tibias *cenac diktbur
varzur kandash"*]
P.T.-J.D. 57 verso
Provenance: Luis Cardoza y Aragon,
Mexico
Exhibited: 1987, Paris, no. 26, ill.
p. 31; 1995, Marseille, no. 31, ill p. 125
Musée National d'Art Moderne—
Centre de Création Industrielle,
Centre Georges Pompidou, Paris

22
*"La révolte des anges sortis des
limbes"* [The revolt of the angels
exited from limbo]
c. January–February 1946
Graphite and wax crayon
25½ x 19⅝" (65 x 50 cm)
Signed lower right, not dated;
inscribed "la révolte des anges /
sortis des limbes" ["the revolt of
the angels exited from limbo"]
ex P.T.-J.D.
Provenance: Gaston Ferdière,
Matarasso, Tristan Tzara
Exhibited: 1995, Marseille, no. 34,
ill. p. 129
Musée Cantini, Marseille

23
"La bouillabaisse de formes dans la tour de babel" [The bouillabaisse of forms in the tower of Babel]
c. February 1946
Graphite and wax crayon
24⅞ x 18⅞" (63 x 48 cm)
Not signed, not dated; inscribed: "La bouillabaisse de / formes / dans / la tour de / babel" ["The bouillabaisse of forms in the tower of Babel"]
P.T.-J.D. 59
Provenance: Marcel Bisiaux
Exhibited: 1980, Les Sables d'Olonne, no. 10; 1987, Paris, no. 28; 1995, Marseille, no. 36, ill. p. 133
Private collection

24
"La maladresse sexuelle de dieu" [The sexual awkwardness of god]
c. February 1946
Graphite and wax crayon
24⅞ x 19½" (63 x 49 cm)
Signed lower right, not dated; inscribed: "La maladresse sexuelle / de dieu" ["The sexual awkwardness of god"]
P.T.-J.D. 60
Provenance: Marcel Bisiaux
Exhibited: 1980, Les Sables d'Olonne, no. 11; 1987, Paris, no. 29, ill. p. 37; 1995, Marseille, no. 37, ill. p. 135; 1995, Paris, no. 7, ill. p. 75
Private collection

25
"Le théâtre de la cruauté" [The theater of cruelty]
c. March 1946
Graphite and wax crayon
24¾ x 18⅛" (62 x 46 cm)
Signed lower right, not dated; inscribed: "Catherine / le theatre de / la cruauté" ["Catherine the theater of cruelty"]
P.T.-J.D. 62
Provenance: Paule Thévenin
Exhibited: 1947, Paris; 1987, Paris, no. 30; 1994, Paris; 1995, Marseille, no. 39, ill. p. 141
Musée National d'Art Moderne— Centre de Création Industrielle, Centre Georges Pompidou, Paris. Bequest of Paule Thévenin, 1993

26
The Inca (L'Inca)
c. March 1946
Graphite and wax crayon
25¼ x 18⅞" (64 x 48 cm)
Signed lower right, not dated; inscribed: "Elah"
P.T.-J.D. 63
Provenance: Paule Thévenin
Exhibited: 1947, Paris; 1987, Paris, no. 32; 1994, Paris; 1995, Marseille, no. 38, ill. p. 139
Musée National d'Art Moderne— Centre de Création Industrielle, Centre Georges Pompidou, Paris. Bequest of Paule Thévenin, 1993

27
Man and His Pain
(L'Homme et sa douleur)
c. April 1946
Graphite and wax crayon
25½ x 15¼" (65 x 38.5 cm)
Signed lower right, not dated
P.T.-J.D. 64
Provenance: Jacques Latrémolière; Hôtel Drouot, Paris, 1 October 1990; Joshua Mack, New York
Exhibited: 1995, Marseille, no. 41, ill. p. 145
Musée Cantini, Marseille

28
Death and Man
(La Mort et l'homme)
c. April 1946
Graphite and wax crayon
25⅞ x 20" (65.5 x 50.5 cm)
Signed lower right, not dated
P.T.-J.D 65
Provenance: Gaston Ferdière; Matarasso; Irène Nomikosoff
Exhibited: 1987, Paris, no. 33, ill. p. 41; 1995, Marseille, no. 42, ill. p. 147
Musée National d'Art Moderne— Centre de Création Industrielle, Centre Georges Pompidou, Paris. Gift of Michel Ellenberger, 1988

29
"L'exécration du Père-Mère" [The execration of the Father-Mother]
April 1946
Graphite and wax crayon
25¾ x 19¾" (64.5 x 49.5 cm)
Signed and dated lower right; inscribed: "l'exécration / du Père-Mère" ["the execration of the Father-Mother"]
P.T.-J.D. 67
Provenance: Jean Paulhan; Jacques Moussempès
Exhibited: 1947, Paris; 1974, Paris, no. 439; 1979, Paris, no. 5; 1980, Les Sables d'Olonne, no. 8; 1981, Paris, no. 42, ill. p. 156; 1987, Paris, no. 34, ill. p. 39; 1993, Paris, no. 1000; 1995, Marseille, no. 43, ill. p. 151; 1995, Paris, no. 6, ill. p. 74
Musée National d'Art Moderne— Centre de Création Industrielle, Centre Georges Pompidou, Paris

30
The Whisk (La Balayette)
[5] May 1946
Graphite
26½ x 19⅝" (67 x 50 cm)
Signed and dated lower right
P.T.-J.D. 68
Exhibited: 1947, Paris; 1987, Paris, no. 36, ill. p. 42; 1995, Marseille, no. 45, ill. p. 155
Private collection

31
Earth's Bodies (Les Corps de terre)
3 May 1946
Graphite and wax crayon
25¾ x 19⅞" (65.5 x 50.5 cm)
Signed and dated lower right;
inscribed: "A Madame Madeleine
Dequeker à / qui la mort aussi a pris
chaque jour / plus d'un crâne et qui
de plus en plus / s'en souviendra"
["To Madame Madeleine Dequeker
for whom death has also taken each
day more than a skull and who will
more and more remember it"]
P.T.-J.D. 66
Provenance: Madeleine Dequeker
Exhibited: 1987, Paris, no. 35; 1995,
Marseille, no. 44, ill. p. 153
Musée National d'Art Moderne—
Centre de Création Industrielle,
Centre Georges Pompidou, Paris

33
The Blue Head (La Tête bleue)
c. May 1946
Graphite and wax crayon
24⅞ x 18⅞" (63 x 48 cm)
Signed lower right, not dated;
inscribed: "Yvonne / Anie /
Catherine / Cécile / Elah / Ana /
[glossolalia]"
P.T.-J.D. 70
Provenance: Paule Thévenin
Exhibited: 1947, Paris; 1987, Paris,
no. 38; 1994, Paris, ill.; 1995,
Marseille, no. 46, ill. p. 157; 1995,
Geneva, no. 20, ill. p. 77
Musée National d'Art Moderne—
Centre de Création Industrielle,
Centre Georges Pompidou, Paris.
Bequest of Paule Thévenin, 1993

35
Portrait of Jacques Prevel
27 August 1946
Graphite
11 x 8⅞" (28 x 22.5 cm)
Signed lower right, dated lower left
P.T.-J.D. 73
Provenance: Rolande Ibrahim Prevel
Exhibited: 1947, Paris; 1976, Paris,
ill. p. 192; 1980, Les Sables d'Olonne,
no. 3; 1990, Saint-Etienne, no. 1,
ill. p. 29; 1995, Marseille, no. 49,
ill. p. 165
Musée Cantini, Marseille

37
Portrait of Sima Feder
7 October 1946
Graphite
24⅞ x 18⅞" (63 x 48 cm)
Signed and dated lower center
P.T.-J.D. 78
Exhibited: 1947, Paris; 1967, Paris;
1976, Paris, ill. p. 145; 1977, London,
no. 103; 1980, Les Sables d'Olonne,
no. 5; 1995, Marseille, no. 53,
ill. p. 171
Collection Florence Loeb

32
Self-Portrait
11 May 1946
Graphite
24⅞ x 19½" (63 x 49 cm)
Signed and dated lower right
P.T.-J.D. 69
Provenance: Gaston Ferdière;
Marcel Bisiaux
Exhibited: 1980, Les Sables d'Olonne,
no. 1, ill.; 1987, Paris, no. 37; 1990,
Saint-Etienne, no. 3, ill. p. 30; 1995,
Marseille, no. 47, ill. p. 159
Private collection

34
Portrait of Rolande Prevel
20 August 1946
Graphite
10½ x 8⅝" (27 x 22 cm)
Signed lower right, not dated
P.T.-J.D. 72
Provenance: Rolande Ibrahim Prevel
Exhibited: 1947, Paris; 1980, Les
Sables d'Olonne, no. 2; 1981, Paris,
no. 55, ill. p. 157; 1987, Paris, no. 39;
1995, Marseille, no. 48, ill. p. 163
Musée Cantini, Marseille

36
Portrait of Pierre Loeb
6 October 1946
Graphite
10½ x 8⅛" (27 x 20 cm)
Signed and dated lower right
P.T.-J.D. 76
Exhibited: 1947, Paris; 1967, Paris;
1976, Paris, ill. p. 146; 1979, Paris, no.
7, ill. p. 11; 1980, Les Sables d'Olonne,
no. 4; 1981, Paris, no. 44, ill. p. 157;
1995, Marseille, no. 52, ill. p. 169;
1996, Tanlay
Collection Florence Loeb

38
M. Victor
5 November 1946
Graphite
25¼ x 19½" (64 x 49 cm)
Signed and dated lower right
P.T.-J.D. 80
Provenance: Colette Allendy
Exhibited: 1947, Paris; 1977, London,
no. 114; 1981, Paris, no. 46, ill. p. 146;
1987, Paris, no. 41, ill. p. 43; 1995,
Marseille, no. 54, ill. p. 173
Private collection

39
Portrait of Roger Blin
22 November 1946
Graphite
29 x 20⅞" (74 x 53 cm)
Signed and dated lower right
P.T.-J.D. 81
Provenance: Paule Thévenin
Exhibited: 1987, Paris, no. 42; 1994,
Paris; 1995, Marseille, no. 55,
ill. p. 175
Musée National d'Art Moderne—
Centre de Création Industrielle,
Centre Georges Pompidou, Paris.
Bequest of Paule Thévenin, 1993

40
Portrait of Florence Loeb
4 December 1946
Graphite
26⅝ x 20⅞" (68 x 53 cm)
Signed and dated lower right
P.T.-J.D. 82
Exhibited: 1947, Paris; 1967, Paris;
1976, Paris, ill. p. 147; 1977, London,
no. 104; 1979, Paris, no. 8, ill. p. 57;
1980, Les Sables d'Olonne, no. 6;
1981, Paris, no. 45, ill. p. 156; 1987,
Paris, no. 43; 1990, Saint-Etienne,
no. 2, ill. p. 26; 1995, Marseille,
no. 56, ill. p. 177
Collection Florence Loeb

41
Self-Portrait
17 December 1946
Graphite
24¾ x 18⅛" (62 x 46 cm)
Signed and dated lower right
P.T.-J.D. 83
Provenance: Pierre Loeb
Exhibited: 1947, Paris; 1967, Paris;
1974, Paris, no. 440; 1976, Paris, ill.
p. 143; 1977, London, no. 101, ill.;
1979, Paris, no. 12, ill. p. 57; 1980,
Les Sables d'Olonne, no. 7, ill.; 1981,
Paris, no. 43, ill. p. 13; 1983, Paris,
no. 1001; 1987, Paris, no. 44; 1990,
Saint-Etienne, no. 5, ill. p. 27; 1995,
Marseille, no. 57, ill. p. 179; 1996,
Tanlay
Collection Florence Loeb

42
Portrait of Domnine Thévenin
7 March 1947
Graphite
25½ x 20⅞" (65 x 53 cm)
Signed and dated lower right
P.T.-J.D. 85
Provenance: Paule Thévenin
Exhibited: 1987, Paris, no. 46; 1994,
Paris; 1995, Marseille, no. 60,
ill. p. 183
Musée National d'Art Moderne—
Centre de Création Industrielle,
Centre Georges Pompidou, Paris.
Bequest of Paule Thévenin, 1993

43
Portrait of Marcel Bisiaux
25 April 1947
Graphite
22 x 17¼" (56 x 44 cm)
Signed and dated lower right
P.T.-J.D. 86
Exhibited: 1947, Paris; 1980,
Les Sables d'Olonne, no. 17; 1990,
Saint-Etienne, no. 7, ill. p. 26; 1995,
Marseille, no. 59, ill. p. 181
Private collection

44
Portrait of Jacques Prevel
26 April 1947
Graphite
25 x 19⅛" (63.5 x 48.5 cm)
Signed and dated lower center;
inscribed: "Si Jacques Marie Prevel
pouvait savoir quel Péché / l'écrase,
et moi, qui ne crois pas au Péché /
je dis de quel / Péché mis sur lui
Jacques Prevel écrase / Que Jacques
Marie Prevel ne fasse pas le / Péché
que toute sa figure médite, qu'en / lui
Marie prémédite contre Jacques
Prevel / L'Androgyne / rompu /
reprit / l'un / et / le / tenta / de /
l'homme / mais / c'est / qu'il / le /
tentait / de / la / femme / dans /
le / même / moment / et / Satan /
le / fou / fut / partout." ["If Jacques
Marie Prevel could know what Sin
overwhelms him, and me, who does
not believe in Sin, I can say what Sin
cast on Jacques Prevel overwhelms
him, may Jacques Marie Prevel not
commit the Sin that his entire face
meditates, may the Mary [Marie]
within him premeditate against
Jacques Prevel. The shrewd

Androgyne tempted him as a man
but at the same time tempted him as
a woman, and Satan the jester was
everywhere."]
P.T.-J.D. 87
Provenance: Jany Seiden de Ruy
Exhibited: 1947, Paris; 1981, Paris,
no. 52, ill. p. 41; 1987, Paris, no. 48;
1993, Paris, no. 1004; 1995, Marseille,
no. 61, ill. p. 185; 1995, Venice,
no. VI.4, ill. p. 373
Musée National d'Art Moderne—
Centre de Création Industrielle,
Centre Georges Pompidou, Paris

45
Portrait of Paule Thévenin
27 April 1947
Graphite
28¾ x 21" (73 x 53 cm)
Not signed, not dated
P.T.-J.D. 89
Provenance: Paule Thévenin
Exhibited: 1987, Paris, no. 48; 1994,
Paris; 1995, Marseille, no. 62,
ill. p. 187
Musée National d'Art Moderne—
Centre de Création Industrielle,
Centre Georges Pompidou, Paris.
Bequest of Paule Thévenin, 1993

46
Portrait of Minouche Pastier
May 1947
Graphite
29¼ x 20½" (74.5 x 52 cm)
Signed and dated lower center
P.T.-J.D. 90
Provenance: Paule Thévenin
Exhibited: 1987, Paris, no. 49;
1994, Paris; 1995, Marseille, no. 65,
ill. p. 193

Musée National d'Art Moderne—
Centre de Création Industrielle,
Centre Georges Pompidou, Paris.
Bequest of Paule Thévenin, 1993

47
Portrait of Mania Oïfer
May 1947
Graphite
25¼ x 20⅞" (64 x 53 cm)
Signed and dated lower right
P.T.-J.D. 91
Provenance: Albert Loeb
Exhibited: 1947, Paris; 1976, Paris,
ill. p. 142; 1977, London, no. 106;
1979, Paris, no. 10, ill. p. 56; 1980, Les
Sables d'Olonne, no. 19; 1981, Paris,
no. 51, ill. p. 156; 1987, Paris, no. 50;
1995, Marseille, no. 63, ill. p. 189
Musée Cantini, Marseille

48
Portrait of Jacques Prevel in Profile
11 May 1947
Graphite
22⅛ x 17⅝" (56.5 x 45 cm)
Signed and dated lower right
P.T.-J.D. 92
Provenance: Rolande Ibrahim Prevel
Exhibited: 1947, Paris; 1980,
Les Sables d'Olonne, no. 21; 1987,
Paris, no. 51; 1995, Marseille, no. 64,
ill. p. 191
Musée Cantini, Marseille

49
Portrait of Colette Thomas
21 May 1947
Graphite
25½ x 19⅝" (65 x 50 cm)
Signed and dated lower right
P.T.-J.D. 94
Exhibited: 1947, Paris; 1995,
Marseille, no. 66, ill. p. 195
Private collection

50
Portrait of Minouche Pastier
22 May 1947
Graphite and wax crayon
25 x 18⅞" (63.5 x 47.8 cm)
Signed and dated lower right
P.T.-J.D. 95
Exhibited: 1947, Paris; 1981, Paris,
no. 49, ill. p. 156; 1987, Paris, no. 52,
ill. p. 45; 1995, Marseille, no. 67,
ill. p. 197
Musée National d'Art Moderne—
Centre de Création Industrielle,
Centre Georges Pompidou, Paris

51
Portrait of Paule Thévenin or *Paule
with Irons* (*Paule aux ferrets*)
24 May 1947
Graphite and wax crayon
25¼ x 20¾" (64 x 52.5 cm)
Signed and dated lower right;
inscribed: "Je mets ma / fille en
sentinelle / elle est fidèle / car
Ophélie s'est levée tard." ["I posted
my daughter as a sentinel, she is
faithful for Ophelia has risen late."]
P.T.-J.D. 96
Provenance: Paule Thévenin
Exhibited: 1947, Paris; 1987, Paris,
no. 53; 1994, Paris; 1995, Marseille,
no. 68, ill. p. 199
Musée National d'Art Moderne—
Centre de Création Industrielle,
Centre Georges Pompidou, Paris.
Bequest of Paule Thévenin, 1993

52
Portrait of Arthur Adamov
c. 17 June 1947
Graphite and wax crayon
26½ x 21½" (67 x 54 cm)
Signed lower right, not dated;
inscribed: "Arthur Adamov / auteur /
de / *l'aveu* / livre unique / dans
l'histoire / des 'lettres'." ["Arthur
Adamov author of *L'Aveu* (*The
Confession*), a unique book in the
history of 'letters'."]
P.T.-J.D. 97
Exhibited: 1947, Paris; 1967, Paris;
1976, Paris, ill. p. 141; 1977, London,
no. 105; 1980, Les Sables d'Olonne,
no. 23; 1987, Paris, no. 54; 1995,
Marseille, no. 69, ill. p. 201; 1996,
Tanlay
Collection Florence Loeb

53
Portrait of a Man
c. 20 June 1947
Graphite and wax crayon
24 x 18⅞" (61 x 48 cm)
Not signed, not dated; inscribed:
"Quel art! / J'ai attendu toute la soirée
des / visites qui ne sont pas venues; /
par contre j'ai re- / çu la visite d'un
Robert Michelet / et d'un de ses amis
qui fout en / l'air l'ésotérisme. Ce /
portrait est / celui d'un / prisonnier
de / la Santé" ["What art! I waited
all evening for visitors who never
came; however I received the visit of
one Robert Michelet and one of his
friends who absolutely negates
esoterism. This portrait is that of a
prisoner of La Santé"]
P.T.-J.D. 98
Exhibited: 1987, Paris, no. 55; 1995,
Marseille, no. 70, ill. p. 202
Private collection

54
Portrait of Lily Dubuffet
22 June 1947
Graphite and wax crayon
26¼ x 19¼" (67 x 49 cm)
Signed and dated lower center
ex P.T.-J.D.
Exhibited: 1995, Marseille, no. 72,
ill. p. 205
Private collection

55
Portrait of Yves Thévenin
24 June 1947
Graphite and wax crayon
25 ½ x 19 ¾" (65 x 50 cm)
Signed and dated lower right;
inscribed: "cesar darvi cesar
dararvi sharva"
P.T.-J.D. 99
Provenance: Paule Thévenin
Exhibited: 1947, Paris; 1987, Paris,
no. 56; 1994, Paris; 1995, Marseille,
no. 71, ill. p. 203; 1995, Venice, VI. 2,
ill. p. 374
Musée National d'Art Moderne—
Centre de Création Industrielle,
Centre Georges Pompidou, Paris.
Bequest of Paule Thévenin, 1993

56
Portrait of Jany de Ruy
2 July 1947
Graphite and wax crayon
25 ½ x 19 ⅝" (65 x 50 cm)
Signed and dated lower center;
inscribed: "Voici un / dessin / qui /
outrepasse / et de / loin / Léonard /
de Vinci / or ce n'est / pas surtout par
/ le dessin par le / tout / de l'autre /
. . . / encore trop [jeune pour] avoir /
des rides. [Je fais ces] enfants / de
rides pauvres, et je les envoie com- /
battre dans mon corps. / Seulement /
je manque d'énergie et cela / se voit;
et je suis encore / terriblement
romantique / comme ce dessin qui
me / répresente, en fait, trop bien, /
et je suis faible, une faiblesse. / et qui
/ aujourd'hui / dira / quoi? / Saint /
Antonin." ["Here is a drawing that

goes beyond, far beyond, Leonardo da
Vinci, but it's not especially in the
drawing in the ensemble of the other
. . . still too [young to] have wrinkles.
[I beget these] children from poor
wrinkles, and I send them to do battle
within my body. Only I lack energy
and that is evident; and I am still
terribly romantic like this drawing
which represents me, in fact, too well,
and I am weak, a weakness. and who
today will say what? Saint Antonin."]
P.T.-J.D. 101
Provenance: Jany Seiden de Ruy
Exhibited: 1976, Paris, ill. p. 139;
1987, Paris, no. 58, ill. p. 47; 1990,
Saint-Etienne, no. 9, ill. p. 31; 1995,
Marseille, no. 74, ill. p. 211
Musée National d'Art Moderne—
Centre de Création Industrielle,
Centre Georges Pompidou, Paris

57
Portrait of Colette Thomas
c. August 1947
Graphite
23 ¼ x 17 ⅝" (59 x 45 cm)
Not signed, not dated; inscribed:
"[glossolalia]"
P.T.-J.D. 102
Provenance: Paule Thévenin
Exhibited: 1987, Paris, no. 59; 1994,
Paris; 1995, Marseille, no. 75, ill.
p. 213; 1995, Venice, VI. 3, ill. p. 375
Musée National d'Art Moderne—
Centre de Création Industrielle,
Centre Georges Pompidou, Paris.
Bequest of Paule Thévenin, 1993

58
Portrait of Colette Allendy
25 August 1947
Graphite and wax crayon
25 ½ x 19 ⅝" (65 x 50 cm)
Signed and dated lower center
P.T.-J.D. 103
Provenance: Paule Thévenin
Exhibited: 1987, Paris, no. 60; 1994,
Paris; 1995, Marseille, no. 76, ill.
p. 215
Musée National d'Art Moderne—
Centre de Création Industrielle,
Centre Georges Pompidou, Paris.
Bequest of Paule Thévenin, 1993

59
Portrait of Alain Gheerbrant
c. November 1947
Graphite
13 ⅞ x 19 ⅞" (34.8 [left side],
32.4 cm [right side] x 50.3 cm)
Not signed, not dated
P.T.-J.D. 104
Exhibited: 1990, Saint-Etienne,
no. 8, ill. p. 28; 1996, Antibes
Private collection

60
Portrait of Henri Pichette or *Gris-gris*
21 November 1947
Graphite
25 ¼ x 19 ¾" (64.7 x 49.8 cm)
Signed and dated lower left
P.T.-J.D. 105
Provenance: Henri Pichette
Exhibited: 1976, Paris, ill. p. 144;
1987, Paris, no. 61, ill. p. 51; 1990,
Saint-Etienne, no. 10, ill. p. 32; 1993,
Paris, no. 1003; 1995, Marseille,
no. 77, ill. p. 217
Musée National d'Art Moderne—
Centre de Création Industrielle,
Centre Georges Pompidou, Paris

61
Portrait of Georges Pastier
December 1947
Graphite
17 ⅝ x 13 ¾" (45 x 35 cm)
Not signed, not dated
P.T.-J.D. 106
Provenance: Paule Thévenin
Exhibited: 1994, Paris; 1995,
Marseille, no. 79, ill. p. 219
Musée National d'Art Moderne—
Centre de Création Industrielle,
Centre Georges Pompidou, Paris.
Bequest of Paule Thévenin, 1993

62
Self-Portrait
c. December 1947
Graphite
14½ x 10½" (37 x 27 cm)
Not signed, not dated
P.T.-J.D. 107
Provenance: Jacques Donnars
Exhibited: 1967, Paris; 1976, Paris,
ill. p. 2; 1980, Les Sables d'Olonne,
no. 16, ill.; 1981, Paris, no. 54; 1987,
Paris, no. 62; 1990, Saint-Etienne,
no. 4, ill. p. 29; 1995, Marseille,
no. 78, ill. p. 218
Collection Florence Loeb

64
Self-Portrait
December 1947
Graphite
25½ x 19⅝" (65 x 50 cm)
Signed and dated lower center
(misdated 1948)
P.T.-J.D. 109
Provenance: Paule Thévenin
Exhibited: 1987, Paris, no. 64, ill.
p. 53; 1994, Paris; 1995, Marseille,
no. 82, ill. p. 225
Musée National d'Art Moderne—
Centre de Création Industrielle,
Centre Georges Pompidou, Paris.
Bequest of Paule Thévenin, 1993

66
Untitled
c. January 1948
Graphite
25½ x 19⅝" (65 x 50 cm)
Not signed, not dated; inscribed:
"[glossolalia]"
P.T.-J.D. 111
Provenance: Paule Thévenin
Exhibited: 1987, Paris, no. 66, ill.
p. 55; 1994, Paris; 1995, Marseille,
no. 83, ill. p. 227
Musée National d'Art Moderne—
Centre de Création Industrielle,
Centre Georges Pompidou, Paris.
Bequest of Paule Thévenin, 1993

Musée National d'Art Moderne—
Centre de Création Industrielle,
Centre Georges Pompidou, Paris.
Bequest of Paule Thévenin, 1993

68
Untitled
c. February 1948
Graphite
25½ x 19⅝" (65 x 50 cm)
Not signed, not dated
P.T.-J.D. 116
Provenance: Paule Thévenin
Exhibited: 1987, Paris, no. 68; 1994,
Paris; 1995, Marseille, no. 85,
ill. p. 231
Musée National d'Art Moderne—
Centre de Création Industrielle,
Centre Georges Pompidou, Paris.
Bequest of Paule Thévenin, 1993

63
Faces
c. December 1947
Graphite
25¼ x 20⅛" (64 x 51 cm)
Signed lower left, not dated;
inscribed: "à Florence la Pauvre / qui
elle aussi se révoltera." ["to Florence
the Poor Thing who will also
revolt."]
P.T.-J.D. 108
Exhibited: 1967, Paris; 1976, Paris,
ill. p. 138; 1977, London, no. 107, ill.;
1979, Paris, no. 14, ill. p. 57; 1980,
Les Sables d'Olonne, no. 22, ill.; 1987,
Paris, no. 63; 1990, Saint-Etienne,
no. 6, ill. p. 32; 1995, Marseille,
no. 81, ill. p. 223
Collection Florence Loeb

65
The Projection of the True Body
(*La Projection du véritable corps*)
18 November 1946–December 1947
or January 1948
Graphite and wax crayon
21¼ x 29½" (54 x 75 cm)
Signed and dated lower right;
inscribed: "[glossolalia]"
P.T.-J.D. 110
Provenance: Paule Thévenin
Exhibited: 1987, Paris, no. 65; 1994,
Paris; 1995, Marseille, no. 80,
ill. p. 221
Musée National d'Art Moderne—
Centre de Création Industrielle,
Centre Georges Pompidou, Paris.
Bequest of Paule Thévenin, 1993

67
Untitled
c. January 1948
Graphite
25½ x 19⅝" (65 x 50 cm)
Not signed, not dated; inscribed:
"Vous avez étranglé et asphyxié
Yvonne / Allendy et elle a été mise
au / cercueil avec le cou le cou le cou
/ marbré de taches noires / et cela
diable ne s'oublie pas cela / diable ne
/ s'oublie pas. . . . [glossolalia]"
["You have strangled and
asphyxiated Yvonne Allendy and she
has been placed in a coffin with the
neck the neck the neck marbled with
black spots and that will not be
forgotten, will not be forgotten."]
P.T.-J.D. 112
Provenance: Paule Thévenin
Exhibited: 1987, Paris, no. 67; 1994,
Paris; 1995, Marseille, no. 84,
ill. p. 229

Man Ray
Antonin Artaud
1926
Gelatin-silver print
9¼ x 7" (23.4 x 17.8 cm)
The Museum of Modern Art
Gift of Paul F. Walter

Chronology

1896   4 SEPTEMBER: Born Antoine Marie Joseph Artaud in Marseille, the first of nine children of Antoine Roi Artaud and Euphrasie Nalpas, whose mothers were sisters. Two siblings survive infancy: Marie-Ange (1898–1986) and Fernand (1907–1989). Antonin's father is a ship builder; his mother, from Smyrna, is of Greek origin.

1901   Has severe attack of meningitis and consequently will suffer from acute headaches, nervous disorders, stammering, and fatigue throughout adolescence.

1905   Deeply affected by death of his seven-month-old sister, Germaine. Christened a Catholic, he is enrolled in Collège du Sacré-Coeur, a Marist academy.

1906   SUMMER: First of several stays in Smyrna with maternal grandmother, Marie Nalpas. Learns to speak fluent Greek and Italian.

1910   Begins writing poetry under pseudonym Louis des Attides. Publishes poetry journal with classmates.

1913   Reads Baudelaire, Rimbaud, and Poe. Considers becoming a priest.

1914–15   Suffering depression, burns his poetry, gives away his books, and leaves school before the *baccalauréat;* sent to a sanatorium, La Rouguière, near Marseille.

1916   SEPTEMBER: Drafted into military service, stationed at Digne, in the south of France; discharged on 20 January 1917 for health reasons. Poems published in *Revue de Hollande.*

1917   Undergoes rest-cures at St. Dizier, near Lyon; Lafoux-les-Bains; and Divonne-les-Bains. Diagnosed with hereditary syphilis and given massive doses of arsenic, bismuth, and mercury.

1918–19   Transfers to Le Chanet, sanatorium in Neuchâtel, Switzerland, and remains there for over a year. Laudanum, an opiate, is prescribed, initiating life-long drug addiction. Begins painting and drawing.

1920   MARCH: Moves to Paris under care of Dr. Édouard Toulouse, head of Villejuif asylum, known for his interest in mechanisms of genius and nervous disorders of artists. Lodges briefly with Toulouse family, then begins nomadic existence, staying in hotels and with acquaintances. Becomes managing editor of Toulouse's literary journal *Demain* and writes art and theater criticism. Trains as actor with director Lugné-Poë.
AUTUMN: Meets poet Max Jacob and painter Elie Lascaux, who introduce him to Daniel-Henry Kahnweiler, André Masson, Joan Miró, Tristan Tzara, and Roger Vitrac.

1921   SEPTEMBER: Joins company of Charles Dullin at his theater, L'Atelier. Besides acting, designs sets and costumes.
AUTUMN: Meets Génica Athanasiou, Romanian actress in Dullin's company; their romantic involvement lasts intermittently until 1927.

1922   Accepts several roles in Dullin's productions.
NOVEMBER: Signs contract with Kahnweiler to publish group of poems, *Backgammon of Heaven.*

1923   APRIL: Leaves L'Atelier and joins company of Georges and Ludmilla Pitöeff. Submits poems to *La Nouvelle Revue Française* and corresponds with its editor, Jacques Rivière, who refuses his poems but publishes their letters as *Une Correspondance avec Jacques Rivière* (1924). Organizes, writes, and publishes two issues of magazine *Bilboquet.*
MAY: At Masson's studio on the Rue Blomet, meets Jean Dubuffet, Michel Leiris, and Georges Limbour.

1924   Begins film-acting career with encouragement from uncle Louis Nalpas, a leading producer. Appears in *Fait-Divers,* directed by Claude Autant-Lara.
19 APRIL: Publishes first important essay about theater, "The Evolution of Décor," in *Comoedia.*
AUTUMN: Invited by André Breton to join Surrealists; introduced to Louis Aragon, Robert Desnos, Max Ernst, Benjamin Péret, and Phillipe Soupault.
7 SEPTEMBER: Death of father.

Antonin Artaud in Marseille, 1918.

1925   23 JANUARY: Becomes director of Central Bureau for Surrealist Research and produces issue no.3 of *La Révolution Surréaliste*.
JULY: Publication of *The Umbilicus of Limbo*, with frontispiece, a portrait of Artaud, by Masson, and *The Nerve Meter*, with cover by Masson. Develops close friendship with Vitrac. Writes three screenplays, not published or produced in his lifetime.

1926   APRIL: Publication of "Fragments of a Diary from Hell" in *Commerce*.
AUTUMN: Writes "Manifesto for a Theater That Failed" and formulates plans for Alfred Jarry Theater, named after eccentric French playwright who wrote *Ubu Roi* (1896). With financial support for project from Dr. René Allendy and his wife Yvonne, Alfred Jarry Theater stages four productions before folding in 1929. Meets and is photographed by Man Ray.
DECEMBER 10: Expelled from Surrealist group. Breton, Aragon, Paul Eluard, and Péret publish pamphlet vilifying Artaud, *Au grand jour* [In the Light of Day].

1927   MARCH: In Marseille undergoes first of many detoxification attempts.
APRIL: Writes screenplay *The Seashell and the Clergyman*. Strongly disagrees with Germaine Dulac's direction of film.
APRIL: Release of *Napoléon*, directed by Abel Gance; role as Marat makes him a celebrity.
JUNE: In response to expulsion from Surrealist movement, publishes pamphlet *In Total Darkness, or The Surrealist Bluff*.

1928   9 FEBRUARY: At première of *The Seashell and the Clergyman*, Artaud and friends provoke a brawl, protesting the film.
APRIL: Release of *The Passion of Joan of Arc*, directed by Carl Dreyer, with Artaud as the monk Massieu.

1929–30 Intense involvement with cinema projects.

1931   JULY: Attends performance of Balinese dancers at Colonial Exposition in Paris; deeply affected, writes essay about the dance for *La Nouvelle Revue Française*.
NOVEMBER–DECEMBER: Invited by Dr. Allendy, delivers lecture at the Sorbonne, "Mise en Scène and Metaphysics."

1932   OCTOBER: *The Theater of Cruelty* (first manifesto) published in *La Nouvelle Revue Française*. Collaborates with André Gide on an adaptation of *Arden of Feversham*.
DECEMBER: Enters clinic in Paris to undergo detoxification.

1933   FEBRUARY: Publication of second Theater of Cruelty manifesto. Writes scenario *The Conquest of Mexico*.
MARCH: Meets Anaïs Nin, who assists him in establishing the Theater of Cruelty.
6 APRIL: Gives lecture at the Sorbonne, "The Theater and the Plague."

1934   APRIL: Writes preface to catalogue for Balthus exhibition at Galerie Pierre.
Publishes *Heliogabalus, or The Anarchist Crowned*.
OCTOBER: Begins writing *The Cenci*, adapted from Shelley and Stendhal.
DECEMBER: Gallimard accepts *The Theater and Its Double* for publication.

1935   6–23 MAY: Directs and acts in *The Cenci*. Balthus designs costumes and sets. Artaud's most ambitious theater project is a financial and critical failure. Meets writer Marthe Robert, establishing a lifelong friendship. Jean Paulhan replaces Rivière as editor of *La Nouvelle Revue Française* and becomes Artaud's friend and supporter.

AUGUST: Death of Yvonne Allendy.
OCTOBER: Meets Cécile Schramme, a young Belgian artist.

1936   6 JANUARY: Departs for Mexico, via Antwerp and Cuba, on board the SS *Albertville*. In Havana, takes part in voodoo ceremony; silver dagger given to him by sorcerer-priest later appears in several drawings (e.g., cat. no. 10).
FEBRUARY: In Mexico City, meets painters Diego Rivera and Maria Izquierdo and writer Luis Cardoza y Aragon. Lectures on "Surrealism and Revolution," "Man Against Destiny," and "Theater and the Gods" at University of Mexico. Publishes articles and reviews in local press.
SUMMER: Travels to Sierra Madre in northern Mexico; stays among Tarahumara Indians and participates in peyote rituals. Profoundly marked by the experience, writes *A Voyage to the Land of the Tarahumara*.
OCTOBER: Returns to France, via Chihuahua and Vera Cruz, where he embarks on the SS *Mexique*.
12 NOVEMBER: Arrives in Paris.

1937   JANUARY: Reunited with Schramme, makes plans for marriage.
APRIL: Undergoes detoxification at clinic in Sceaux. Acquires wooden cane said to have been owned by St. Patrick and ascribes to it magical powers. After reconciliation with Breton, frequents his Gradiva gallery.
MAY: Gives scandalous lecture in Brussels, "The Decomposition of Paris." Engagement to Schramme is broken off by her parents.
JUNE: Writes *The New Revelations of Being*.
10 AUGUST: Abruptly departs for Ireland to return St. Patrick's cane to the people of Ireland and to discover the lost rites of the Celts.
AUGUST–SEPTEMBER: Arrives at the port of Cobh and journeys to Galway, the Aran Islands, and then Dublin. Sends series of spells to recipients including Lise Deharme and Jacqueline Breton (cat. nos. 2 and 3).
SEPTEMBER: With no money or access to drugs, and unable to communicate in English, becomes increasingly unstable and is arrested on several occasions for public disturbances in Dublin. His cane is confiscated.
23 SEPTEMBER: Confined in Mountjoy prison as arrangements are made to deport him.
29 SEPTEMBER: Departs from Cobh on board the SS *Washington*. Allegedly attacks two mechanics on board with his Cuban dagger and is forcibly restrained. Arrives in Le Havre bound in a straightjacket and is transported to Quatre-Mares psychiatric hospital near Rouen.

1938   12 APRIL: Transferred to Sainte-Anne Hospital in Paris, where his illness is diagnosed as "incurable paranoid delirium"; begins eight-year internment in a series of psychiatric hospitals.
FEBRUARY: *The Theater and Its Double* is published by Gallimard.

1939–43   Confined in Ville-Évrard, large psychiatric hospital near Paris. Outbreak of World War II in September 1939 results in severe shortages of food and medicine. Suffers physical and medical neglect and psychological condition deteriorates. Sends spells to recipients including Léon Fouks, Sonia Mossé, Roger Blin, and Adolf Hitler (cat. nos. 4–7).

1943   FEBRUARY: Concerned about his condition, Desnos and Artaud's mother arrange his transfer to Rodez, a psychiatric hospital 372 miles south of Paris, in the unoccupied zone. Spends three-week interim at psychiatric hospital of Chezal-Benoît. At Rodez he is patient of Dr. Gaston Ferdière, pioneer of electro-shock therapy, poet, and friend of the Surrealists.
JUNE: Subjected to first sequence of three electroshocks, his vertebrae are fractured. Given private room and takes meals with Dr. Ferdière; condition rapidly improves but he remains in precarious state and suffers frequent fits of delirium. Encouraged to read, write, and draw.
OCTOBER: Subjected to second sequence of twelve electroshocks. Begins to lose teeth as a result of treatment. Undertakes an adaption of Lewis Carroll's *Through the Looking Glass*.

Antonin Artaud, 1946.
Photographed by Denise Colomb.

1944   Begins to draw using graphite and wax crayons and paper given to him by local painter, Frédéric Delanglade (cat. nos. 11–33). Undertakes translations of Keats and adaptions of Poe poems, including *Annabel Lee* and *Israfel*. Begins writing and drawing in notebooks.
23 MAY – 10 JUNE: Subjected to third series of twelve electroshocks.
AUGUST: Subjected to fourth series of twelve electroshocks.
DECEMBER: Subjected to fifth series of twelve electroshocks. In all, received fifty-one electroshocks over a nineteen-month period.

1945   End of World War II brings visits to Rodez from friends, including Arthur Adamov, Blin, Dubuffet, and Robert. Allowed to come and go from the hospital, he makes plans to leave and return to Paris.
AUGUST: Learns of deaths of Desnos and Mossé in concentration camps.
NOVEMBER: Publication of *A Voyage to the Land of the Tarahumara*.

1946   MAY: Dr. Ferdière releases Artaud into the care of his friends on condition that he has financial security and remains under medical supervision. Adamov appoints Paule Thévenin, a medical student, to arrange for a room at the private Ivry-sur-Seine clinic run by Dr. Achille Delmas.
7 JUNE: Constitution of a committee of friends to find financial support for Artaud. Breton opens benefit-performance of Artaud's writings at the Sarah Bernhardt Theater, organized by Adamov and Jean-Louis Barrault.
13 JUNE: Auction of manuscripts and paintings arranged by Adamov at the Galerie Pierre on behalf of Artaud. With donations from Georges Bataille, Simone de Beauvoir, Georges Braque, Dubuffet, Pablo Picasso, Jean-Paul Sartre, and others, a sum of more than one million francs is raised, which is administered by Dubuffet and later by Pierre Loeb.
16 JULY: Records "Insanity and Black Magic" for French radio.
AUGUST: Begins series of portraits of friends and acquaintances, including Rolande and Jacques Prevel (cat. nos. 34, 35), Dubuffet, and Robert.
SEPTEMBER: Stays in Sainte-Maxime, in south of France, with Robert. Writes *Artaud le Mômo*.
AUTUMN: Makes portraits of Blin (cat. no. 39), Sima Feder (cat. no. 37), Jacques Germain, Florence Loeb (cat. no. 40), Pierre Loeb (cat. no. 36), and Mania Oïfer.

1947   13 JANUARY: Gives three-hour performance at Vieux-Colombier Theater in Paris, *Tête à tête, par Antonin Artaud* [Face to Face with Antonin Artaud], reading poems and texts.
FEBRUARY: Visits an exhibition of van Gogh's paintings at the Orangerie, and writes *Van Gogh: The Man Suicided by Society*.
SPRING: Makes portraits of Marcel Bisiaux (cat. no. 43), Minouche Pastier (cat. nos. 46 and 50), Jacques Prevel (cat. nos. 44 and 48), and Thévenin (cat. nos. 45 and 51), as well as self-portraits.
JULY: Exhibition at Galerie Pierre, *Portraits et dessins par Antonin Artaud* [Portraits and Drawings by Antonin Artaud], for which he writes catalogue preface, "The Human Face" (see pp. 94–97). Writes two long poems, published together as *Ci-gît, précédé de La Culture indienne* [Here Lies, preceded by Indian Culture]. Compiles texts for publications *Suppôts et suppliciations* [Fragmentations and Interjections]. Keeps notebooks, in which he composes poetry, draws, and makes notes.
NOVEMBER – JANUARY 1948: Records *To Have Done with the Judgment of God* for radio transmission. The canceling of the program by the director of French Radio the day before its scheduled broadcast creates public controversy.
Artaud's health deteriorates; takes large doses of heroin, chloral hydrate, and cocaine to combat pain of as-yet-undiscovered rectal cancer.

1948   FEBRUARY: Diagnosed with advanced, inoperable rectal cancer.
4 MARCH: Dies at the age of fifty-two at Ivry.

Interior of Artaud's room in the psychiatric clinic in Ivry-sur-Seine, 1947. Photographed by Denise Colomb.

Exhibition History

1947 *Portraits et dessins par Antonin Artaud*. Galerie Pierre, Paris, 4–20 July. Catalogue; preface by Artaud.

1966 *Antonin Artaud, Max Ernst, Henri Michaux*. Le Point Cardinal, Paris, March–April.

Dessins de poètes. Le Bateau Lavoir, Paris, April. Catalogue.

Phantastische Kunst, Surrealismus. Kunsthalle, Bern, 21 October–4 December. Catalogue.

1967 *Antonin Artaud*. L'Atelier, Paris.

1973 *Antonin Artaud*. Bibliothèque Municipale, Rodez, May.

1974 *Jean Paulhan à travers ses peintres*. Grand Palais, Paris, 1 February–15 April. Catalogue; essay by André Berne Joffroy.

1976 *Artaud*. Librairie-Galerie Obliques, Paris, autumn. Catalogue published in *Obliques*, 1976, no. 10–11; includes essays by Arthur Adamov, Michel Camus, Jérôme Prieur, and Michel Sicard.

1977 *Antonin Artaud and After*. National Book League, London, 19 October–12 November. Checklist in Ronald Hayman, *Artaud and After* (London: Oxford University Press, 1977).

Chemins de la création. Chateau, Ancy-le-Franc.

1979 *L'Aventure de Pierre Loeb: La Galerie Pierre, Paris, 1927–1964*. Musée d'Art Moderne de la Ville de Paris, 7 June–16 September, and Musée d'Ixelles, Brussels, 4 October–23 December. Catalogue; essay by André Berne Joffroy.

1980 *Antonin Artaud (1896–1948), dessins*. Musée de l'Abbaye Sainte-Croix, Les Sables d'Olonne, 5 July–30 September. Catalogue in *Cahiers de l'Abbaye Sainte-Croix*, no. 37; essays by Henry-Claude Cousseau, Jean-Louis Schefer, and Paule Thévenin.

1981 *Paris-Paris, 1937–1957*. Musée National d'Art Moderne, Centre Georges Pompidou, Paris, 28 May–2 November. Catalogue; essays relating to Artaud by Agnès de la Beaumelle, André Berne Joffroy, and Sarah Wilson.

1984 *Écritures dans la peinture*. Villa Arson, Nice, April–June. Catalogue; essay by Paule Thévenin.

1987 *Antonin Artaud, dessins*. Musée National d'Art Moderne, Centre Georges Pompidou, Paris, 30 June–11 August. Catalogue; essay by Paule Thévenin.

1989 *Un Certain Regard des années 50*. Saarland Museum, Saarbrücken, Germany, 30 April–25 June. Catalogue; essay by Paule Thévenin.

1990 *L'Ecriture griffée*. Musée d'Art Moderne de Saint-Etienne, 6 December–25 February. Catalogue; essays by Bernard Ceysson and Jacques Beauffet.

1993 *L'Âme au corps: Arts et sciences 1793–1993*. Grand Palais, Paris, 19 October–24 January, 1994. Catalogue; essay by Jean Clair.

1994 *Dessins d'Antonin Artaud, reçu en legs de Paule Thévenin*. Musée National d'Art Moderne, Centre Georges Pompidou, Paris, 14 September–31 October. Catalogue.

1995 *Antonin Artaud: Oeuvres sur papier*. Musée Cantini, Marseille, 17 June–17 September. Catalogue; essays by Agnès de la Beaumelle, Nicolas Cendo, Jean-Michel Rey, and Jean-Louis Schefer.

Féminin-masculin, le sexe de l'art. Musée National d'Art Moderne, Centre Georges Pompidou, Paris, 24 October–12 February 1996. Catalogue; essays by Marie-Laure Bernadac and others.

Identity and Alterity: Figures of the Body 1895/1995. 46 Esposizione Internazionale d'Arte, Biennale, Venice, June–September. Catalogue; essays by Jean Clair and others.

1945 Les Figures de la liberté. Musée Rath, Geneva, 27 October–7 January 1996. Catalogue; essays by Claire Stoullig and others.

1996 *Hommage à Denise Colomb*. Centre d'Art Tanlay, 18 May–20 October.

1946. Musée Picasso, Antibes, 28 June–30 September.

One-person exhibition

Select Bibliography

Antonin Artaud's writings are collected in his *Oeuvres complètes,* edited by Paule Thévenin, in twenty-six volumes (Paris: Editions Gallimard, 1956–94). References to it in this book are abbreviated as *O.C.,* followed by the volume and page numbers. Unless otherwise noted, the most recent edition of the *Oeuvres complètes* is cited.

By Artaud

ENGLISH TRANSLATIONS OF ARTAUD'S WRITINGS

Eshleman, Clayton, trans., with Bernard Bador. *Watchfiends and Rack Screams: Late Writings of Antonin Artaud.* Boston: Exact Change, 1995.

Eshleman, Clayton, and Norman Glass, trans. *Antonin Artaud: Four Texts.* Los Angeles: Panjandrum Books, 1986.

Hirschman, Jack, ed. *Antonin Artaud: An Anthology.* San Francisco: City Lights, 1965.

Sontag, Susan, ed., and Helen Weaver, trans. *Selected Writings of Antonin Artaud.* New York: Farrar, Straus & Giroux, 1976.

Writings by Artaud about His Drawings

"Ce dessin est une sensation qui a passé en moi…" (1946). *O.C.* 21, 180–82. About *Death and Man,* cat. no. 28.

"Ce dessin est une tentative grave…" (1946). *O.C.* 19, 259–60. About *The Machine of Being,* cat. no. 21 (verso).

"Ce dessin ne s'adresse donc pas…" (1946). *O.C.* 21, 186. About *Death and Man,* cat. no. 28.

"50 Dessins pour assassiner la magie" (January 1948). See pages 32–37.

"Dix ans que le langage est parti…" (April 1947). *Luna Park,* October 1979.

"Les figures sur la page inerte…" (April 1947). *Antonin Artaud:*

Oeuvres sur papier, 90. Marseille: Musée Cantini, 1995. See page 42.

"L'Homme et sa douleur" (1946). *O.C.* 14, 46–47 and 205–6. About *Man and His Pain,* cat. no. 27.

"Il ne s'agit pas de créer un métalloïde…" (1946). *O.C.* 21, 223–24. About *Death and Man,* cat. no. 28.

"Je me souviens dans une existence perdue…" (1945). *O.C.* 18, 73–74. About *Couti l'anatomie,* cat. no. 15.

"Mes dessins ne sont pas des dessins mais des documents…" (1946). *O.C.* 21, 266–67. See pages 61–62.

"La Mort et l'homme" (1946). *O.C.* 21, 157. About *Death and Man,* cat. no. 28.

"La mort et l'homme…" (1946). *O.C.* 21, 232–33. About *Death and Man,* cat. no. 28.

"Le tombeau de tout qui attend…" (1946). *O.C.* 20, 170–73. About *"La maladresse sexuelle de dieu,"* cat. no. 24.

"Le visage humain est une force vide…" Preface to *Portraits et dessins par Antonin Artaud.* Paris: Galerie Pierre, 1947. See pages 94–97.

Writings by Artaud about Art

"A propos des Indépendants, du cubisme et de quelques autres…" ("L'Expression aux Indépendants") (1921). *O.C.* 2, 171–75.

"L'Art et la mort" (1929). *O.C.* 1, bk. 1, 140–42.

"Le Cubisme, les valeurs picturales et le Louvre" (1921). *O.C.* 2, 186–87.

"Le Dernier Aspect du Salon" (1921). *O.C.* 2, 198–200.

"Exposition Balthus à la Galerie Pierre" (1934). *O.C.* 2, 242–44.

"Exposition Kisling" (1924). *O.C.* 2, 220.

"L'Expression aux Indépendants." See "A propos des Indépendants…"

"La Figure du Salon d'automne" (1920). *O.C.* 2, 167–70.

"Franz Hals" (1936). *O.C.* 8, 245–46.

"La Jeune Peinture française et la tradition" (1936). *O.C.* 8, 201–6.

"Lettre de Paris: Exposition Picasso" (1924). *O.C.* 2, 219.

"Lugné-Poë et la peinture" (1921). *O.C.* 2, 188.

"Le Mexique et l'esprit primitif: Maria Izquierdo" (1937). *O.C.* 8, 258–63.

"La Mise en scène et la métaphysique" (1932). *O.C.* 4, 32–45.

"Paul les Oiseaux ou La Place de l'amour" in *L'Ombilic des limbes* (1925). *O.C.* 1, bk. 2, 9–15. About Paolo Uccello.

"Un Peintre mental" (1923). *O.C.* 1, bk. 1, 240. About Paul Klee and Georg Grosz.

"La Peinture de Maria Izquierdo" (1936). *O.C.* 8, 252–55.

"Les Salons du printemps, La Nationale" (1921). *O.C.* 2, 189–90.

"Texte surréaliste" (1925). *O.C.* 1, bk. 2, 18–19. About André Masson.

Van Gogh, le suicidé de la société (1947). *O.C.* 13, 13–64.

"Visite au peintre Fraye" (1921). *O.C.* 2, 184–85.

On Artaud

MONOGRAPHS

André-Carraz, Danièle. *L'Expérience intérieure d'Antonin Artaud.* Paris: Librairie Saint-Germain-des-Prés, 1973.

Barber, Stephen. *Antonin Artaud: Blows and Bombs.* London and Boston: Faber & Faber, 1993.

Brau, Jean-Louis. *Antonin Artaud.* Paris: La Table Ronde, 1971.

Charbonnier, Georges. *Essai sur Antonin Artaud.* Paris: Seghers, 1959. Reprint, 1970.

Greene, Naomi. *Antonin Artaud: Poet without Words.* New York: Simon and Schuster, 1970.

Hahn, Otto. *Portrait d'Antonin Artaud.* Paris: Le Soleil Noir, 1968.

Hayman, Ronald. *Artaud and After.* London: Oxford University Press, 1977.

Knapp, Bettina. *Antonin Artaud: Man of Vision.* Preface by Anaïs Nin. New York: Discus, 1969.

Lévêque, Jean-Jacques. *Antonin Artaud.* Paris: Henri Veyrier, 1985.

Maeder, Thomas. *Antonin Artaud.* Paris: Plon, 1978.

Mèredieu, Florence de. *Antonin Artaud, les couilles de l'ange.* Paris: Blusson, 1992.

Prevel, Jacques. *En compagnie d'Antonin Artaud.* 2d ed. Paris: Flammarion, 1994.

Thévenin, Paule. *Antonin Artaud, ce désespéré qui vous parle.* Paris: Seuil, 1993.

White, Kenneth. *Le Monde d'Antonin Artaud.* Paris: Editions Complexe, 1989.

Special Periodical Issues Dedicated to Artaud

Arts (Paris), November 1958.

L'Autre Journal, 1993, no. 1.

Cahiers de la Pléiade, no. 7 (spring 1949).

Les Cahiers du Chemin, no. 19 (October 1973).

Cahiers Renaud-Barrault de la Compagnie Madeleine Renaud–Jean-Louis Barrault, nos. 22–23 (May 1958). Reprint, no. 69 (1969).

Entretiens, 1979.

Europe, nos. 667–668 (November–December 1984).

France-Asie, no. 30 (September 1948).

K, 1948, nos. 1–2 (June).

Le Magazine Littéraire, no. 61 (February 1972).

———, no. 206 (April 1984).

Obliques, nos. 10–14 (4th trimester, 1976).

Obsidiane, no. 5 (March 1979).

Planète Plus, no. 7 (February 1971).

84, 1948, nos. 5–6.

Tel Quel, no. 20 (winter 1965).

———, no. 39 (autumn 1969).

———, no. 40 (winter 1970).

La Tour de Feu, nos. 63–64 (December 1959). Reprints, nos. 112 (December 1971) and 136 (1977).

Essays about Artaud's Drawings

Barber, Stephen. "Cruel Journey." *Art in America*, February 1995: 71–75.

———. "A Foundry of the Figure: Antonin Artaud." *Artforum* 26, no. 1 (September 1987): 88–95.

Derrida, Jacques. "Forcener le subjectile." In *Antonin Artaud: Dessins et portraits.* Paris: Gallimard; Munich: Schirmer-Mosel Verlag, 1986.

Mèredieu, Florence de. *Antonin Artaud: Portraits et gris-gris.* Paris: Blusson, 1984.

———. "Artaud/Balthus: Peinture et mise en scène." *Cahiers du Musée National d'Art Moderne*, 1983, no. 12: 217–23.

———. "Les Dessins d'Artaud." *La Nouvelle Revue Française*, no. 301 (February 1978): 164–66.

Rey, Jean-Michel. "Poétique de la peinture . . ." In *Antonin Artaud: Oeuvres sur papier.* Marseille: Musée Cantini, 1995.

Schefer, Jean-Louis. ". . . cet essoufflement de la conscience . . ." In *Antonin Artaud: Oeuvres sur papier.* Marseille: Musée Cantini, 1995.

———. "Dessins d'Artaud." *Café*, 1983, no. 3: 117–20.

Thévenin, Paule. "Antonin Artaud, autoportrait." *Artpress*, no. 101 (March 1986): 76–77.

———. "Antonin Artaud (1896–1948), dessins." *Cahiers du Musée de l'Abbaye Sainte-Croix*, no. 37 (1980): 5–7.

———. "Dessin à regarder de traviole." *Café*, 1983, no. 3: 121.

———. "Un Insurgé de l'art." In *Antonin Artaud: Dessins.* Paris: Centre Georges Pompidou, 1987.

———. "La Maladresse sexuelle de dieu." *Peinture/Cahiers Théoriques*, 1971, no. 1: 33–42.

———. "La Recherche d'un monde perdu." In *Antonin Artaud: Dessins et portraits.* Paris: Gallimard; Munich: Schirmer-Mosel Verlag, 1986.

Weiss, Allen S. "Innate totems: Artaud's Drawings." In *Perverse Desire and the Ambiguous Icon.* Albany: State University of New York Press, 1994.

Reference Publications

Bersani, Leo. "Artaud, Defecation and Birth." In *A Future for Astyanax: Character and Desire in Literature.* Boston: Little, Brown, and Co., 1969.

Deleuze, Gilles. "The Schizophrenic and Language: Surface and Depth in Lewis Carroll and Antonin Artaud." In Josué Harari, ed., *Textual Strategies in Post-Structuralist Criticism.* Ithaca: Cornell University Press, 1979.

Derrida, Jacques. "The Theater of Cruelty and the Closure of Representation" and "La Parole Soufflé." In *Writing and Difference.* Chicago: University of Chicago Press, 1978.

Foucault, Michel. "The Birth of the Asylum." In Richard Howard, trans., *Madness & Civilization: A History of Insanity in the Age of Reason.* New York: Vintage Books, 1965.

Lotringer, Sylvère. "Antonin Artaud." In *European Writers: The Twentieth Century*, vol. 2. New York: Charles Scribner's Sons, 1988.

Robert, Marthe. "Je suis cet insurgé du corps." *Cahiers de la Compagnie Madeleine Renaud–Jean-Louis Barrault*, nos. 22–23 (May 1958): 49–60.

———. "Le Retour de Rodez." In *La Traversée littéraire.* Paris: Grasset, 1994.

Sontag, Susan. "Approaching Artaud." *The New Yorker*, 19 May 1973: 39–78.

Todorov, Tzvetan. "Art According to Artaud." In *Poetics of Prose.* Ithaca: Cornell University Press, 1977.

Wilson, Sarah. "From the Asylum to the Museum: Marginal Art in Paris and New York, 1938–68." In *Parallel Visions: Modern Artists and Outsider Art.* Los Angeles: Los Angeles County Museum of Art, 1992.

Photograph Credits

Trustees of The Museum of Modern Art

Antonin Artaud, 1947. Photographed by Georges Pastier.